HOT FLASHES, WARM BOTTLES

hot flashes
warm bottles

FIRST-TIME MOTHERS OVER FORTY

NANCY LONDON, M.S.W.

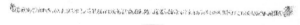

CELESTIAL ARTS
Berkeley / Toronto

A Kirsty Melville Book

Celestial Arts
PO Box 7123
Berkeley, California 94707
www.tenspeed.com

Distributed in Australia by Simon and Schuster Australia, in Canada by
Ten Speed Press Canada, in New Zealand by Southern Publishers Group, in
South Africa by Real Books, in Southeast Asia by Berkeley Books, and in the
United Kingdom and Europe by Airlift Book Company.

Library of Congress Cataloging-in-Publication Data
London, Nancy, 1944–
Hot flashes, warm bottles : first-time mothers over forty / Nancy London.
        p. cm.
"A Kirsty Melville book"—Verso t.p.
Includes bibliographical references and index.
ISBN 0-89087-971-0
1. Middle aged mothers—United States—Psychology. 2. Middle aged
mothers—United States—Attitudes. 3. Middle aged mothers—United States—
Social Conditions. I. Title.
HQ759.43 .L66   2001
306.874'3—dc21   2001028128

Cover design by Jennifer Barry
Text design by Betsy Stromberg

First printing, 2001
Printed in the United States of America

1 2 3 4 5 6 7 8 9 10 — 05 04 03 02 01

For Richard and Sasha,
safe place, true love.

Contents

Acknowledgments

This book would not have been possible without all the first-time mothers over forty who so warmly and generously shared their stories with me and with each other in support groups. Thank you from the bottom of my heart. I made no effort to scientifically analyze my data, nor did I make use of any control groups. As is fairly typical among women, an informal network grew, and one first-time mother referred me to another. Although in most cases I did not use real names, the heart and soul of each woman shines through nonetheless. It is my hope that within the details of these stories the reader will experience that shock of recognition that makes the personal universal. Sometimes in our isolation it's hard to believe that anyone else could feel what we're feeling; it was my intention in writing this book to dispel any such doubts.

A special thanks to Christy Shepard and Wendy Trayberg for their sensitive and valuable contributions to this book.

A heartfelt thank you to my talented literary agent, Jandy Nelson, who knew this book needed to be written and held my hand every step of the way with support, guidance, and always just the right word of understanding and encouragement.

To Kirsty Melville and Holly Taines White at Ten Speed Press, deepest appreciation for your vision and professionalism in helping to make this book all it could be.

Bouquets of gratitude to:

Kimberly Carter, for thirty years of best gal pal friendship, for reading the first draft of this book, and for providing unerring good advice on balancing work and family;

Laura Davis, seasoned author, who was willing to read several drafts of my book and share her humor, encouragement, and professional opinions, despite the fact that she was in the middle of writing her own;

Jane Mattes, for generously connecting me to her Single Mothers by Choice network;

Helen Fabel and Cindy Geist, for reading the first draft of this book and offering suggestions that only first-time moms over forty could provide;

Libby Sternberg, for being such a first-rate networker and mentor for my daughter;

Julie Rivers and Dona Wilder at the Heyokah Retreat Center, LaDonna Knudsen, and Madelaine Goulard, all for opening up their sacred spaces to me when I needed to retreat and write;

Leslie Nathanson, for being such a big-hearted friend to my daughter, and such a source of laughter and comfort to me;

Donna Thomson, for generously making her channeled awareness sessions available when I needed them the most;

Phyllis Leavitt, Joan Schutz, and Keffi Bell, for first-rate friendship for this first-time mom;

Cindy Jurling, for the music and dance she has shared with my daughter;

And to the memory of Fran Clayton.

A special thanks to my mother, Lois, and my brother, Alan, who made my life as a stay-at-home author more comfortable.

Love to my stepdaughter, Shauna, who is a treasured member of our family and much adored big sister.

Love and gratitude to my daughter, Sasha: you were the answer to my heart's deepest prayer and have brought more laughter and pure joy into my life than I ever thought possible.

And finally to my husband, Richard, who read every word of this book and made invaluable suggestions, who cooked nourishing meals for my body and soul, who kept me warm at night, and who, after fourteen years of marriage, is still the kindest, wisest, and most big-hearted person I have ever known. Thank you for your love that never fails.

Too Tired to Be the Tooth Fairy

Motherhood is the most emotional experience of one's life. One joins a kind of women's mafia.

JANET SUZMAN

The need for this book became apparent to me the night I fell asleep from sheer exhaustion before I could leave my nine-year-old daughter, Sasha, a gift from the tooth fairy. I loved being the tooth fairy when she was little, and I used to keep a stash of gifts on hand for these times. I especially enjoyed writing and decorating letters to her from the tooth fairy, admiring her tooth, and telling her how proud I was of her. We had our routine. Sasha would leave her tooth and a note to the fairy, often with a small token of affection, like a seashell or bead, and I would replace her offering with mine. So it was a huge jolt to me the morning my daughter came sobbing into the kitchen because the tooth fairy hadn't come. She felt abandoned and betrayed by her friend from the spirit world who had, up until now, delivered some pretty fair booty. "Good grief," I thought, abashed and a little alarmed, "I'm too tired to be the tooth fairy."

After five emotionally devastating and physically depleting miscarriages in my thirties, I had given birth to my first and only child three months shy of my forty-fourth birthday. At the time, I felt young, vital, and capable of juggling parenting, marriage, and a fulfilling career as a therapist specializing in women's issues. Now, nine years later, I was struggling with exhaustion, impatience, irritability, and a growing desire for solitude.

What happened to my intention to be the Perfect Mother? The Perfect Mother was patient. *She* didn't resort to yelling. *She* didn't have violent mood swings. But I did. Unlike a younger mother, my fantasies and expectations of myself and the virtues I would bring to parenting had had decades to solidify; now my inability to live up to this self-created myth was causing me secret shame and confusion. And so I took courage and my own good advice as a therapist and began to explore and accept all the conflicting voices clamoring inside of me.

In the hopes of finding some confirmation that I wasn't cracking up in my own private universe, I started searching bookstores for clues—had other women ever felt what I was feeling? I started with books on motherhood, but they offered no insight. What I found next astonished me: Everything I had been feeling—peace, grief, teeth-clenching impatience, cell-tingling joy, bone-deep exhaustion (often all in one day), all the nameless yearning, ambivalence, body changes—they were all described exactly as I was experiencing them in books *by women going through menopause.* I was elated. I had stumbled out of my own dark room into a brilliantly lit banquet hall. I was entering menopause but had been too busy raising a young child to notice! Certainly finding this confirmation and reassurance was the "good news." The "bad news" was that all these books were written for women whose children were already grown. The self-help suggestions were geared toward women who had large chunks of discretionary time they could lavish on themselves: time to retreat and nurture oneself during periods of heightened fatigue and irritability, time to explore new avenues of creativity in silence, time and space for artful flower arrangements in pristine environments long beyond needing to be "kid proof." In short, these books assumed I had time to journey through the midlife transition focused wholly on a new set of developmentally appropriate needs and desires. "But what about me?" I heard myself almost bleat in the bookstore. "What about *my* transition that includes these needs and desires *and* a small child that I adore?"

We learn best to listen to our own voices if we are listening at the same time to other women, whose stories—for all our differences— turn out, if we listen well, to be our stories also.

BARBARA DEMING

Suspecting that I wasn't alone in this dilemma, I ran a small ad in the local paper seeking first-time moms over forty interested in forming a support group to explore the spiritual, emotional, and physical challenges of raising children as mature women. For the next ten days, I was deluged with phone calls from dozens of older mothers. When these women realized that I wanted to explore both the joys *and* the challenges of parenting at our age, they cried, begged, and bribed to attend. The night of our first support group I came prepared, like a good therapist, with several ice-breaking exercises. But before I could pass out name tags, before they had their coats off, they were sharing their experiences as older mothers with each other in the deepest, most intimate fashion imaginable.

Since that night, I have been privileged to hear the stories of countless other older mothers ranging in age from forty to sixty, with children six months to sixteen years old. These women are either married or single, are lesbian or straight, gave birth or adopted, work inside or outside the home, used infertility treatments to conceive or conceived naturally, or started second families after forty. We are as much unlike younger mothers as we are unlike older mothers with grown children.

In those early support groups, several issues were raised over and over again. These issues provide the framework for this book:

- Older mothers may enter perimenopause soon after giving birth, and the developmentally appropriate needs that surface for her at this time are often at odds with the developmentally appropriate needs of her young child. This is what I call the "Clash of the Titans."

- The older woman who gives birth in her forties undergoes a rapid and potentially disturbing shift in self-image, from "I still feel and look like twenty-nine and I'm ready for sex" before childbirth to "How can this be me crawling to bed at nine o'clock in my flannel pajamas?" In many cases, the mothers of her child's friends are ten to fifteen years younger than she is. She feels tired and bedraggled by comparison, and often struggles to maintain her self-esteem and sense of desirability in a culture that worships youth.

- Older mothers often feel forced to choose between a career they have cultivated for decades that may now be in mid-bloom or staying at home with a much anticipated child. This is significantly different from the younger woman who may have worked for only a few years before starting a family and has much less time, identity, and meaning invested in her career.

- Older mothers are often sandwiched between caring for their elderly parents and meeting the needs of their young child. Too often, there's no time or energy left to meet their own needs, and the support their elderly parents might have been able to offer a decade ago is no longer available.

- Because the chances of successfully conceiving decrease with age, many women who postponed having children until their forties are now resorting to a variety of infertility treatments. While the literature focuses on the cutting-edge advances of these technologies, the emotional, psychological, and financial repercussions are often overlooked.

- Increasingly, older women are turning to domestic and foreign adoption as a means of becoming parents. Many of these children are from cultures light-years different from ours, and they are often old enough to have suffered abuse and neglect.

- The psychological and physical demands of successfully ushering a teenager into adulthood are enormous, and no matter how well she takes care of herself, an older mother will be in her fifties when her child is a hormone-driven adolescent.

In addition, I have come to understand that the children of older mothers have very real concerns that they are sometimes reluctant to share, and so I have devoted a chapter to letting the children speak for themselves.

How We Came to Be First-Time Moms over Forty

While the total births for women in the United States have steadily decreased since 1980, they have risen sharply among older women: between 1980 and 1995, the birth rate for women forty to forty-four increased an astonishing 81 percent.

The American College of Obstetricians and Gynecologists estimates that we will have entered the new millennium with one in every twelve babies being born to women aged thirty-five and older.

Several factors have contributed to this extension of a woman's "fertility deadline" from her early thirties to early forties: Our society as a whole is enjoying improved health and extended longevity; women now have reliable birth control and access to legal abortions; and the Women's Movement and the politics of sexual equality encouraged a whole generation of girls to challenge the notion that biology was destiny and to step out of the traditionally defined roles of wife and mother into a brave new world where all things seemed possible.

I made choices as part of the times we lived in. I'm grateful not to have been roped into marriage and motherhood at twenty.

MARIA, FORTY-EIGHT-YEAR-OLD MOTHER OF SIX-YEAR-OLD SAM

Over the last two years, I have interviewed dozens of older first-time moms, always asking how they came to be mothers in their forties rather than their thirties or even twenties, and have found their answers as interesting and varied as the women themselves. Their stories reflect not only their personal circumstances, but also the heady political and social climate of the times in which they came of age.

Lynn told the support group: "Even when I was a kid setting the dinner table, I knew I never wanted to be like my mom. She worked as a secretary all day and then came home and put in another eight-hour shift. She never even had a choice. I resented my dad because of the inequality, because he had the power and his work was valued in the world. Did I want to be powerless or powerful? It was a real no-brainer. The Women's Movement gave me the license to be who I really was and to make the choice not to get married at eighteen. I went into computer science and was the only girl in my class."

June grew up in a small town in the South, and said, "I thought the biggest trap any woman could fall into was being barefoot and pregnant. I was from a lower middle-class family, and there really wasn't anyone in front of me to show me how to go about becoming a professional. I didn't know any women who worked. It took all of my twenties getting up the courage to figure out how to negotiate the academic system to get into medical school." June became a successful pediatrician, married at thirty-eight, and started trying to have a baby six months later. "I thought I was going to get pregnant right away, but it didn't happen. After a year my doctor started a fertility workup and I entered the whole nightmare of infertility. We did temperature, we did timed ovulation, we did hormone injections and several intrauterine inseminations. I was obsessed with having a baby, and it nearly destroyed my marriage. Let's face it . . . if someone had given me a monkey at that point, I would have diapered it and tried to nurse it."

Having a kid in my forties was the best thing that ever happened to me. It moved me from being a self-centered, self-absorbed person into feeling an identity with women all over the world. I joined the human race. It cured me of my feelings of terminal uniqueness.

PAULA, FORTY-FIVE-YEAR-OLD MOTHER OF FIVE-YEAR-OLD NICOLAS

Many women put off childbearing to distance themselves from early family responsibilities. "Growing up in a home run by an alcoholic father and a manic-depressive mother, I was pretty much raising my two younger brothers by the time I was seven," Tracey told the support group. "When I hit eighteen, all I wanted was to be free and to lead my own life. I didn't even think about wanting kids of my own until I was thirty-nine."

And then there are the women who wanted children and started trying to have them in their thirties but couldn't, women who had their fertility compromised by drugs like DES that their mothers took when they were in utero or by contraception like the Dalkon Shield, which caused infections and made conception impossible because of scarring.

Some women postponed motherhood until they had the financial resources to parent alone; some waited while they established themselves more securely in careers. Others didn't even know they were waiting. Mara described herself as caught up in living in the moment. "It never occurred to me to get married and have kids when I was in my twenties. Everyone assumed I was on a fast-track career ladder but I wasn't on *any* ladder; I was blowing in the wind. It felt like fall-out from the Women's Movement—*don't get married, don't* get tied down. I just went from one experience to another until I met my husband when I was thirty-eight."

I have heard many stories from women who wisely postponed motherhood until pressing personal issues were resolved. "I came out as a lesbian in my thirties," Becca offered. "My sexual identity had to be in place before I became a parent." Lisa spent her twenties and thirties "reacting to a lot of trauma from my childhood. I was kind of a lost person, but I didn't know where the pain was coming from. I moved around a lot, living a pretty wild lifestyle. I was consumed with my own healing and was in no shape to raise a child. I was forty-one by the time the intensity of that process subsided."

Some women used their fortieth birthday as a deadline: if Mr. or Ms. Right hadn't shown up by then, they'd pursue motherhood on their own. Others came to motherhood in their forties by way of a midlife passage. Sheila grew up in a Christian Science family, "mind over matter, power of positive

My desire to have a child was a total surprise. I think we're just monkeys that talk, that we're totally ruled by our hormones. All those philosophy books are just rationalizing and covering up our hormonal reactions.

DEBBIE, FORTY-SEVEN-YEAR-OLD MOTHER OF SIX-YEAR-OLD BENJAMIN thinking, that kind of thing," she said speaking softly. "I really believed I could do anything. Even though I was aware of my age chronologically, I thought I could get pregnant any time I wanted to. I'm a lesbian, and I wanted a solid relationship in my life before I began inseminating, but by thirty-eight the right partner hadn't come along. I tried getting pregnant with a known donor, but it didn't work. I spent the next seven years taking hormone shots and trying to conceive, but I still couldn't get pregnant. The doctor finally told me I had old eggs. It was a very intense time for me. I was devastated and went into a terrible depression. That experience marked the end of my feeling invincible."

For Lois, twenty-five years of political activism left her feeling like she had "drastically overestimated the potential for change in the human race." Dissatisfied with work and wondering, "Where am I going to put all this energy I used to put into political causes?" she decided, at forty-five, to adopt a five-year-old boy and make a difference in the life of just one child.

All of these women became first-time mothers over forty. Some conceived the first time they tried, others underwent infertility treatments with mild to severe consequences. Some became parents through adoption with partners, some by choice as single women. What, if anything, do they have in common? They all arrived at motherhood no longer young but not yet old. They were wiser, often less idealistic, and, without exception, filled with a never-ending gratitude for the opportunity, no matter how achieved, to be a mother.

> My advice is to follow your heart. Don't have a child before you're ready for it just because you're young. You will have other resources—heart, wisdom, financial—when you're older, so if you don't feel ready until then, lack of youth won't be that much of a problem.
>
> KATHERINE, FORTY-SIX-YEAR-OLD MOTHER OF THREE-YEAR-OLD JANINE

Ultimately all these women chose motherhood out of instinct, intuition, and a deeply held knowledge that parenting was their heart's desire. Out of the hundreds of first-time moms over forty I have met, I have never spoken with one who regretted her decision. Never. But what I *have* heard is, "Oh my God, if I had only known how exhausted I was going to be, I would have done it sooner." Or, "If I had had my baby earlier, my father would still be alive to meet his grandson." Or, "My infertility treatments cost me my entire life savings. Maybe none of this would have been necessary if I had tried to have kids in my thirties." Or, "I love my daughter. Adopting was the best thing I've ever done. But sometimes I feel really sad thinking about my genetic line coming to an end with me."

These are women reflecting in hindsight on the decision to postpone motherhood until their forties. Lest the scales seemed tipped, what they *also* say in overwhelming numbers is, "Having a baby when I was older was the greatest pleasure of my life." And, "I had less difficulty figuring out what was the priority and what was trivial." And, "I had more realistic expectations, I was more relaxed." And, "I was so much more self-aware than I was in my twenties and thirties. I would have made a lousy parent if I had done it any sooner." They are saying it's a trade-off. For the most part, they are exhausted and pushed to their physical limits, but they also revel in the long-sought experience of being a mother even as they fold like a bad poker hand in the early hours of the night.

People without kids seem to lead more superficial lives. These boys have enriched my life. I look at women I've known for twenty years who decided not to have children and I feel sorry for them. I've definitely had more joy from these children than problems.

LISA, FIFTY-TWO-YEAR-OLD MOTHER OF ELEVEN-YEAR-OLD TWINS, ALDEN AND RYAN

The Consequences of Our Choices

I had the life-changing good fortune of being in the right place at the right time: Cambridge, Massachusetts, during the late sixties. I was invited to join a small group of women gathering together once a week to discuss—radical notion—the unique experience of being a woman. This was the first East Coast women's consciousness-raising group, out of which grew the Boston Women's Health Book Collective and the first edition of *Our Bodies, Ourselves,* of which I was a contributing writer. I mention this so that you will understand that as an early card-carrying member of the Women's Movement, I believed we could have it all, be it all, and do it all. Given that predisposition, it has been a gradual awakening on my part to understand that the choices we make *do* bear consequences, despite what our culture's addiction to immediate gratification would have us believe. Working with older women who postponed childbearing until their forties is a lesson in these natural consequences: fertility and life force irrevocably decline with age. Those women who did conceive consider themselves fortunate, as most of them have friends who weren't so lucky and are now facing a childless

> When a motherhood becomes the fruit of a deep yearning, not the result of ignorance or accident, its children will become the foundation of a new race.
>
> MARGARET SANGER

future. Those who resolved their infertility by adopting say that their inability to conceive, no matter what high-tech treatment they employed or how much money they spent, was their first brush with the real lessons of life: "It doesn't always matter how much you want it. Some things are out of your control."

Several of the stories in the book also deal with abortion and its unforeseen consequences. As young women, we claimed our right to this freedom and polarized our politics against the forces that threatened to limit our personal options.

But denying that there are any ramifications to abortion—approaching it as casually as we would a haircut or the removal of a mole—likewise limits freedom of choice, this time the one that comes from understanding and accepting all of the spiritual, emotional, and physical consequences that are part of such a decision.

It was with great empathy and sadness that I recently read a quote from Germaine Greer, torch-bearing, trail-blazing, rabble-rousing feminist writer of the sixties and beyond who expressed the terrible sorrow she feels now that she is past menopause and any chance for motherhood: "I still have pregnancy dreams," she said in an interview with the British magazine *Aura*, "waiting with vast joy and confidence for something that will never happen."

It is my fervent hope that this book not be used by the "family values" crew as an I-told-you-so sneer to uppity women everywhere. Rather it is my intention to offer support, guidance, advice, and an occasional groan of recognition to women in their forties who are already up to their eyeballs in the experience of being older first-time moms and to provide food for thought to younger women who are currently weighing their options.

CHAPTER ONE

Age, Sex, and the Fortysomething Mama

I don't think of myself as middle aged, although when I think about that logically, if I'm not middle aged now, how long am I going to live?

COLLEEN, FORTY-EIGHT-YEAR-OLD MOTHER
OF SIX-YEAR-OLD ZACK

You've probably noticed: Our society worships thinness, beauty, and youth, and at the feet of these false idols, we tend to regard aging less as a natural process and more as a personal failure to remain young. If a woman's self-worth rests primarily in her appearance and sex appeal, she may find herself at midlife inhabiting a kind of limbo-land. If she turned heads when she was in her prime, now she feels stripped of the personal power and privilege that such youth and beauty bestowed on her, and daily slips into an ever-deepening invisibility where buff young guys call her ma'am. For the woman who has hung the hat of her self-esteem on her looks, this passage from bud to full-blown rose is a land mine of nagging self-doubts and insecurities, compounded by a glaring lack of guidance from any inspiring role models who have made this treacherous journey before her.

Certainly our cultural prejudice against the aging woman, the "crone," predisposes us to view the inevitable signs of aging—lines, wrinkles, loosening skin, maybe even warts and moles—with disgust and perhaps shame. We turn away from the image we see in the mirror, feeling betrayed by our younger self who promised never to leave but now has slipped out silently in the night leaving no forwarding address. If we struggle to "retain our youth" in ways that seek to deny our age, we run the risk of looking foolish, even to ourselves. To all things there is a season, and midlife is without doubt the end of high summer.

Nobody whistles at me on the street anymore, so I've decided to wear comfortable shoes.

KELLY, FORTY-SIX-YEAR-OLD MOTHER OF FOUR-YEAR-OLD ERIC

What can we expect in terms of cultural support? Industries that "attack" aging and coincidentally make billions of dollars in bottom-line profits off these tender female vulnerabilities and insecurities. Cosmetics that will turn back "the ravages of time" and cost a third of the monthly mortgage. Shots and pills that target a libido that may be—God forbid—flagging just a tad. Liposuction to make smooth and firm all the cushiony places that made Grandma cozy. And miracle diets that deplete the midlife woman of those five extra pounds where her body, in its infinite wisdom, is storing the reserve estrogen she just might need for a rainy, strung-out day.

Most of our cultural icons seem as confused and conflicted about the aging process as the rest of us. I have watched Oprah's weight yo-yo up and down for years now. She is one of my heroes, a woman I respect and admire, someone who has the courage to play out her struggles in the public arena, mirroring the confusion most of us feel in private. One minute she is militantly in shape, the poster girl for "just do it"— fighting off the ravages of time, beating off the demons of frumpy, dumpy, and lumpy, and pounding the pavement at 5 A.M. The next minute, she's flirting with what my mother would call "letting herself go." Go where? Into the realm of the comfortably plump, the round, *sigh*, older woman? I approach my TV with trepidation whenever my daughter is catching Oprah's afternoon show. Which Oprah will greet me? Her seemingly sudden shifts from—pardon the pun—one end of the scale to the other affect me deeply. I want her to choose so that we all can choose. Are we fighting the good fight to stay young and thin, or are we succumbing? I want to beg . . . Oprah, *please* make up your mind.

> Taking joy in life is a woman's best cosmetic.
>
> ROSALIND RUSSELL

In all fairness, I am certain there are many women who have wholeheartedly embraced this transition. I am sure there are women who look in the mirror tenderly and with deepest acceptance and affection for their wrinkles, sagging skin, and Greek goddess hips, women who never yearned for a push-up bra or a face-lift, but to tell you the truth, I can only count the ones I know on my fingers and a few of my toes.

Hot Flashes, Warm Bottles

If making the transition out of the bloom of youth into middle age is dizzying and disorienting at best for *any* female in our society, it is even more fraught with contradictions for the fortysomething woman with a young child. Statistically, half of all the women who have hot flashes will begin feeling them while they are still menstruating normally, starting as early as age forty. This of course means that our midlife mama just might be having hot flashes at the same time she's warming a bottle or nursing her baby. Night sweats, heart palpitations, outbursts of temper or tears (or both), migraines, itchy skin, insomnia, and incontinence may also accompany her peri-menopause. Whatever impulse she might have toward surrendering gracefully to the emotional and physical imperatives of aging is strongly undermined by her deep desire to stay looking and feeling as youthful as she can for the sake of her child.

Women come to my support groups grateful for the opportunity to unburden themselves of these incongruities. "I'm lactating and incontinent at the same time," June all but shrieked. "I'm using KY Jelly and changing dirty diapers in the same evening!" That definitely started the ball rolling. Each woman present knew exactly what June was trying to describe: aging is happening too soon, my kids are still young, and I'm too young to be old. "I'm not ready to embrace crone-hood," she yelled, and like a war cry it elicited groans, sighs, howls of sympathy, and stories from other women.

"Okay, listen to this," Debra said. "Yesterday I was reading Dr. Seuss to my daughter and the mailman brought me my introductory offer to join AARP. I felt like the earth was splitting under me. I had one foot over the hill and one foot in the nursery." More confessions: "How the hell can I revel in my wrinkles when I just found out my daughter is lying about my age?" Elaine's thirteen-year-old daughter told her that being in the eighth grade and having the oldest mother was so "awesomely uncool" that she lied and told her friends that her mom was forty, a sleek five years younger than her best friend's mom, and a full eighteen light-years away from the truth.

This is how the conflict feels to Lucinda: at fifty, with a five-year-old daughter, she is blessed with natural dark brown hair and skin that reflects the waters of a good gene pool. "But," she said, "my eyebrows are becoming the real symbol of my struggle with aging. They're sprouting white hairs. Sometimes I pluck them because I think Sophie will feel better if I look younger, and sometimes I keep them because I look so dignified! I want to be recognized as a wise woman, but Sophie is pulling me backward into youth."

Annie captured the ultimate moment of dissonance when she described filling her prescription for the estrogen patch that was to help smooth over her extreme midlife moodiness. "So there I am racing out to the Walgreen's parking lot, ripping open my jeans, and sticking on this patch. It was absurd," she laughed. "I had my *toddler* with me!"

It's not that we didn't know we were going to age, it just always seemed like it would happen some time other than now. Our kids would be grown. They'd be sending us extravagant bunches of flowers for Mother's Day, reminiscing about the good times, the years we had together that prepared them for their current good luck in love and worldly success. We'd be wise, we'd be well off. The money we used to spend on the kids could now be lavished on ourselves—spas, facials, lunch with the girls. We'd have the time to finally learn computer science, hydroponic gardening, sushi making. We'd find renewed sexual vigor, buy lingerie from Victoria's Secret, know what to do for vaginal dryness. If we had to age, it would be with style and panache, grace not grit. We would go gently into the autumn of our lives elegant, rested, and wise. Never did we imagine we'd be expressing milk while we were losing our memory, or watching *Sesame Street* with bifocals.

> My daughters want me to dye my hair, but really, it's time to be proud of my age. I'm coming out as an older parent!
>
> NELLIE, FIFTY-YEAR-OLD MOTHER OF SIX-YEAR-OLD TWINS, AMANDA AND SIERRA

These private, startling moments that alert the midlife mother to the obvious fact that she inhabits two distinct worlds become magnified when she steps outside. There, the inescapable evidence that she is out of sync with the mainstream awaits her, as well as the dawning realization that she can never catch up.

Women who tell me they never thought of themselves as old until they looked in a mirror now have their age reflected back to them in society's mirror. "I had a midlife crisis the first time I took my son to school," Allison told me. She is forty-six years old, with a six-year-old child. "There were all these young mothers there who were either pregnant with their second baby or talking about having another. That's when I started to feel old. They're young and still having kids, and I can't do that anymore."

> Nobody dies from lack of sex. It's lack of love we die from.
>
> MARGARET ATWOOD

Iris is elegant at fifty years old, with long gray hair she wears in a thick braid. She adopted her four-year-old son from India three years ago as a single lesbian mother. Last year she helped organize a playgroup with mixed-age moms, and for the first time, became acutely aware of her age. "The trouble was," she told the support group, "when something spilled or something went wrong, the older mothers didn't get up and do anything about it. When the kids were having trouble or needed something, we just sat there. It was the young mothers—the thirty-year-olds—who got things for the kids or pulled them around the yard in their wagons. We fifty-year-olds, we were tired. We were sitting down. I had never really noticed the difference in age until then."

Ginger's epiphany happened on a bike trail. Last year at forty-nine, she and her husband began an exercise program to lose weight and build the endurance they needed to stay active for their four-year-old daughter. "I was pushing myself to get fit," she told us. "I knew it would help me stay healthy and feel like I could keep up with Hannah. I didn't want her to have a fat, tired mom. Last week we were biking in the mountains. It was one of those days when I felt perky. We stopped to let this woman go by. She was about twenty, pushing two kids in a stroller. Actually she was jogging uphill, pushing the stroller. She had an athletic twenty-year-old body. All of a sudden I felt really old. Her kids were going to have a totally different experience with her physically than Hannah will have with me. I stood there envying her youth and her stamina."

"In Texas, most of the moms I met at day care were twenty-two or twenty-three, and had flat stomachs a week after they had their kids," Madeline laughed. "I can remember all the snide and disparaging remarks I'd make to myself looking at them: 'They must waste all their time exercising,' 'She's skinny now but wait until she turns forty.' One woman in hot mini shorts and a halter top with zero body fat said her baby weighed only five pounds at birth and I remember thinking, 'Yeah, you probably starved yourself and your kid has brain damage because of it.' And then," she added, "she had the nerve to ask me if I was my son's grandmother."

My after-forty face felt far more comfortable than anything I lived with previously. Self-confidence was a powerful beauty potion; I looked better because I felt better. Failure and grief as well as success and love had served me well. Finally, I was tapping into that most hard-won of youth dews: wisdom.

NANCY COLLINS

These stories are filled not only with humor, but with subtle incriminations as well: "My body betrayed me by aging." "Our youth culture has abandoned me. I feel ignored and cast aside, and I'm struggling to maintain my self-esteem." "Help! Nobody told me this was about to happen! Nobody warned me. What do I do?"

The answer emerges for each of us at a different time and pace, but I believe it always involves taking steps toward reclaiming our power, vision, and purpose as midlife women. We yearn to claim the wisdom we know on a cellular level is our birthright, but we have to struggle to honor it in a society that reduces its elders to blithering ineffective caricatures in cartoons and films.

The wisdom and power that is potentially ours at this life transition is enormous. It is, in fact, exactly what our society, which is teetering on the edge of ecological disaster, needs desperately. In many Native American societies, the warriors are prohibited from making war without first being granted permission from their elders. Forget Hollywood's version of Big Male Chief with Headdress. Most often the elders are a council of older postmenopausal women, revered for their vision and capacity to cherish and preserve all of life. But we can only access this power and destiny if we have the courage to face our society's marketing demons that would marginalize us and have us believe aging is ugly, lacking in vitality and wisdom, and is best kept out of sight. When we dare to challenge these assumptions, we help make real the future we yearn to bequeath to our children.

The "G" Word

Mention the word out loud—grandmother—and you are flooded for better or for worse with images from your childhood. The grandmothers of your youth—yours, your friends, those belonging to your distant relatives—were so old as to seem ancient. A breed apart. Moving in the slow lane, life had already happened. Grandmothers were wrinkled, often benign, certainly sexless. Imagine, then, the cognitive dissonance a midlife mama feels when she is mistaken for her child's grandparent. She has come to motherhood at a point in her life when she feels young and vital. Of course, occasionally she'll hear of a high school friend whose kids are off to college or even of a friend who has, in fact, become a grandparent, but for the most part the truth that *she* herself is now old enough to be a grandparent doesn't register on the Richter scale.

Until. Until someone smiles and tells her how lovely her granddaughter is, or coos at her new "grandbaby" and shares photographs of their own, or marvels at how much vitality she and her husband have to share with the grandkids. Confusion. Shock. Disbelief. Who the hell are they talking about?

Pam told the group that when she and her husband adopted their daughter she was forty-four and he was forty-seven, older than either of the birth mother's parents. When Pam and her husband arrived at the hospital the day their daughter was born, the nurse greeted them warmly and asked if it was their first grandchild. Pam remembers feeling embarrassed, confused, and above all stunned into an awareness that she looked her age.

Was I concerned about the inevitable issues of age and mortality when I had my child? No. If I had worried about all those things, I probably wouldn't have done it.

MARTHA, FIFTY-YEAR-OLD MOTHER OF TWO-YEAR-OLD MILLIE

Lucinda, our friend who can't decide whether or not to pluck her white eyebrows, remembers the day after a camping trip when the whole family hadn't showered for a week. "The waitress at the restaurant asked my daughter if she was having fun with her grandparents. I said we were her parents and we were all having a delightful time. I felt bad—really bad—and embarrassed for Sophie and I thought, 'Man, do I look that old today?'"

"I was so shocked when it first happened that I lied," Debra laughed. "I was out with my little girl buying her an Easter outfit. The saleswoman cooed at us and said, 'Oh how sweet, spoiling the granddaughter!' I actually didn't know what she meant for a moment. Then I lowered my voice and whispered, 'Yes, her mother died in a car crash and now I'm raising her.'"

When the jokes die down, and the outrageous revenge fantasies have run their course, I often find that acknowledging the inescapable evidence of aging gives women the freedom to talk about some of their other concerns, specifically a growing desire to slow down, their somewhat restricted options for retirement, and a new sense of their own mortality.

Downshifting

"If we hadn't had a kid so late in life, we could have afforded to retire sooner than we can now," Madeline mused. "When I've had a bad week at the office, I come home and say, 'God, look at how much longer I have to work!'"

Even for women who enjoy their work and have no immediate plans to retire, there is the awareness that the midlife impulse to downshift is at odds with the demands of parenting young children. Elizabeth, a sixty-year-old college professor who is in the thick of raising her fourteen-year-old son, told me, "When it's ten o'clock on Saturday night and my son is out, I want to go to bed but I look around for something to do that's going to keep me up. I remember my parents were up when I got home. I don't want him to come home to a dead house. I want to keep a semblance of life in the house because otherwise it's depressing for him. It's a big struggle. My son needs a lot of active engagement. My need to slow down is completely at odds with the next four years of parenting."

Madeline spoke for the group when she voiced her concerns: "I'm hoping there will be some time toward the end of our lives that my husband and I can have for ourselves, but jeez, what shape will I be in? My parents got to retire in their fifties. We'll be closer to seventy!"

Ticktock. Suddenly midlife mothers are measuring years and milestones. "I'll be sixty-two when my daughter graduates from high school." Their own mothers, who may have looked older than the hills to them when they were children, now appear ridiculously young in retrospect. "I was graduating from college when my mother was my age," said the mother of a toddler. Women wonder if their health will hold up over the next critical twenty or so years as they raise their children, and if they will be around long enough to plan weddings and get to know grandchildren.

Time is fleeting and the evidence is upon us: we are aging. Our bodies are morphing, our libidos are wavering, and men hold doors open for us for all the wrong reasons. Given this realization, some women want to spend every precious moment possible with their child who is growing up at an alarmingly fast rate. For others, the "life is short" realization propels them into living more authentically. They seek to cut through any false sense of familial obligation to the heart of freedom and personal fulfillment. This knowledge of the passage of time offers you the choice to make changes in how you live, moment by moment, and day to day. You might experience a greater sense of urgency for the things that matter most to you as an individual, parent, and partner. You might discover a patience and humor rising to the surface of your heart and mind that was buried in the rush of life. You might do everything differently, or keep everything the same. Either way, living with the awareness of your own mortality holds the potential to renew and enrich your relationship with life.

> We've lost a lot of friends to AIDS who were our peers and contemporaries, so we definitely have a sense of our own mortality. So the aging process, although difficult at times, is really a kind of gift.
>
> LYDIA, FORTY-FIVE-YEAR-OLD MOTHER OF THREE-YEAR-OLD BRAD

Can This Really Be Me?

No discussion of a midlife mother's gains and sacrifices would be complete without talking about the one area most fraught with quicksand changes in self-image and self-esteem—her sexuality.

Or the lack of it. Women who just a heartbeat ago were taking romantic vacations with their partners and who counted themselves happily among the sexually active and adventurous, are now crawling to bed in their flannel pajamas at 9 P.M., lusting after nothing more than sleep. For these women, having a child later in life has exacerbated midlife fatigue. Add to that the physical exhaustion that comes from having her hormones spiking and falling several times a day (or an hour) and we have a midlife mama who may no longer feel like a hot young thing ready to jump in the sack.

"I honestly can't believe what's happened to me sexually," Debra told the group. "Being sexual used to be a huge part of my identity. It's how I related to the world. Now I'm either with my kid or at work all day. Either way, when dinner and story time are over, I'm finished too. More than anything, I don't want anyone making one more demand on me. I know that's not a fair thing to say to my husband, but I can't help it. He doesn't pressure me, but I feel bad for him. It's something I feel guilty about."

The group knew Allison's husband, a musician, was six years her junior. Maybe we thought it exempted her from the I'm-too-pooped-to-care-about-sex club, so we were surprised when she said, "I thought that having a younger husband would be stimulating sexually, but there are times I wish he were older than me. His idea of a good time is hours of lovemaking. I don't have the heart to tell him mine is a lavender bath and ten hours of sleep."

Now that the ice had been broken, Annie was eager to share. "I don't know why having a three-year-old has changed my sexuality so much, but it has," she said. "When I look at

> It's only when we truly know and understand that we have a limited time on earth and that we have no way of knowing when our time is up, that we will begin to live each day to the fullest, as if it was the only one we had.
>
> ELISABETH KÜBLER-ROSS

24

our situation, it shouldn't be that much different than it was before our son was born—he's still in a crib and we don't have to worry about him walking in on us—but everything's changed. I guess I'm not comfortable admitting how tired I am most of the time."

"Sex has always been a complex issue for me," Ginger said. "I was sexually abused by my father when I was quite young, so I grew up believing that I had to be sexual in order to be loved. Now I'm in a good relationship and I rarely feel sexual. Partly it's because I'm exhausted after having a baby two years ago, and partly it's because I feel safe now and don't *have* to be sexual to be loved. That's good, but it's also scary. I see other women eyeing my good-looking husband, and I think, 'Great, here I am in my bunny pajamas at eight at night.' So I had to say to myself, 'Look honey, these pajamas are over the line. Put them in the back of the closet and at least go to bed in a nightgown.' We're going to start small, but we *are* going to start."

And so it is that starting small—in fact, starting at ground zero—is exactly where many midlife mothers begin when it comes to rekindling their waning libido. "I always start out minus one on the scale of desire," Annie laughed. "But once we've made love I'm always glad I did. I usually think, 'Hey, I like this. We ought to do this more often. This isn't drudgery at all!'"

Far from drudgery, good sex can be the antidote to feeling undesirable in the eyes of society and is one sure way to reclaim our sense of worth, beauty, and desirability. Good sex that involves the heart as well as the body connects us back to the passions that can remind us of who we were for the

The birth of our son and the fatigue that followed definitely changed our sex life. Now intimacy means that my husband and I sleep snuggled up together after a hectic day or enjoy a quiet cup of coffee together before the day begins.

HANNAH, FORTY-EIGHT-YEAR-OLD MOTHER OF SIX-YEAR-OLD JEREMY

decades preceding motherhood, and most of the women I counsel find that making the effort is worth it.

Saving Face

Many midlife mamas confess to having toyed with the idea of cosmetic surgery to shore up various sagging body parts. "My stomach looks like the old cat dragging around the house." "I'm beginning to trip over my boobs." "My daughter looked at my wedding picture and said, 'Who's that?'" Older moms are often in the company of younger moms—at preschool, PTA meetings, the pediatrician's, Little League, and Disney matinees—and there is no doubt that there is a temptation for many to surgically remove the signs of age that time has wrought. Those who actually do it say that while they knew it was superficial and temporary, it was the only solution they felt they had to deal privately with our society's very public prejudice against aging and aging women in particular. "If only I could have seen my aging face as beautiful instead of ugly," my client, who opted for surgery, said sadly.

This led me once again to examine the images of female beauty and desirability presented to us by our culture. I was hard-pressed to find images of women at midlife who were aging with any degree of grace and self-assurance, let alone ones with small children in tow. The women in magazines look barely old enough to baby-sit, or they are proud to be fortysomething with their wrinkles and cellulite airbrushed away. It's no wonder we're reluctant to let our true face show. Everyone else seems to be hiding theirs. The good news and the bad news is that since there are no decent role models around, tag, we're it. We now have the opportunity to model aging with grace and acceptance.

But accepting ourselves isn't the same as neglecting ourselves, and so for that reason I have four very practical suggestions for preserving and enhancing your beauty and life force.

Don't diet. I knew you'd like this one. We all know that being overweight isn't good for us and is implicated as a risk factor in a host of diseases. But did you also know that your fat cells will freak out once they get wind of your intention to diet and they will store *everything*, even rice cakes, as fat to compensate for what they perceive to be your desire to kill them? Destroy all the diet books and articles you've collected over the years. Rip them apart page by page. Better yet, burn them in your sink, while chanting, "No!" Instead, figure on eating five smallish meals a day to stabilize your blood sugar and your moods. Add some tofu to your diet if you don't already eat it. It's extremely high in protein and contains phytoestrogens that may offer some protection from breast cancer.

> I want to grow old without face-lifts. They take the life out of a face, the character. I want to have the courage to be loyal to the face I've made.
>
> MARILYN MONROE

Drink at least two quarts of water a day. It's great for keeping your skin moisturized and your tummy full between snacks.

Give in to your food cravings every now and again. Chocolate increases two of the brain chemicals—serotonin and endorphins—responsible for a feeling of well-being, no surprise to many of us. Ignoring these cravings when they first announce themselves often leads to eating more sugar, starch, and fat when our resistance has finally been worn down. Again, no big surprise. Besides, life is short, and chocolate is a little bit of heaven. As Erma Bombeck quipped, "Seize the moment. Remember all those women on the *Titanic* who waved off the dessert cart."

Exercise regularly. I know, you've heard this a thousand times, but bear with me. Midlife women who exercise aerobically gain only half the weight of women who don't exercise. If you're not already in the habit, and the very thought of it sounds like as much fun as a trip to the dentist, here are a few things to consider:

- Exercise actually combats fatigue. It also helps with PMS or menopause, smoothes out stress, and encourages the production of mood-enhancing brain chemicals.

- Exercise boosts the midlife metabolism that is naturally slowing down so that we burn what we eat much more efficiently.

- Exercise builds bone mass and helps to prevent osteoporosis.

If you know all of this and exercise still sounds like punishment, I encourage you to find some form of aerobic movement that is actually *fun* for you and give it a two-month try: gardening, hiking, biking, in-line or roller skating, swimming, dancing, even jumping rope with your child. Walking is great—it's the easiest, cheapest, most readily available form of exercise.

Start by doing any of the above at least three times a week, and I guarantee you'll be hooked on how energetic and frisky you start to feel.

Add five extra minutes every week until you reach your time goal. It will give you an Olympian sense of personal accomplishment and fulfillment that has a way of positively affecting the rest of your life. Personally I cherish my time alone sweating on the treadmill, but many women prefer exercising with a friend or their partner.

Beg, borrow, or steal this time. Use your lunchtime at work or the hour before your partner leaves in the morning. Swap childcare with a friend, hire a sitter from the local college, or strap your child to your chest and take off. Please, please, please give this piece of advice a try.

No one can imagine what it is going to feel like to be middle aged, nor understand the consequences of becoming a parent at that age, least of all the twenty- and thirty-year-olds we used to be. In truth, this inability to take into account the fact that being older will actually *feel* different is part of human nature. Yet despite the flagging energy, the body changes, the unexpected mood swings, and the public and private realizations of a youth now fading, most of the women I have worked with welcome the passage of time and the changes it has brought. They feel infinitely more patient as an older woman, and better equipped psychologically to be a parent; they believe having young children keeps them young in spirit and prevents them from becoming prematurely sedentary and set in their ways; they relish leaving behind the White Rabbit pace at which they used to live and love watching ants climb trees with their kids. These are the moms who may be so tired they wonder how they'll get their kids to baseball practice, but do, and whose desire to participate actively in their kids' lives propel them out of the rocking chair and onto the ski slopes. These are the moms who feel enriched by their children no matter what the sacrifice.

> I think it's easier being an older parent. I have more patience and I know myself better, so I can separate what I'm feeling and why (PMS, bad day at work, fight with the boyfriend, etc.) from what she's doing and why (usually tired or hungry).
>
> GLORIA, FORTY-FIVE-YEAR-OLD MOTHER OF THREE-YEAR-OLD CARRIE

The Journey Book

There will be a section at the end of each chapter where I recommend that you work with a Journey Book, so when you have the time, get yourself a blank notebook, some glue, and some scissors. You'll also need a container, like a box with a lid, a basket, a folder, or a big envelope. Find a place to keep it safe—in a closet, under the bed, in your drawer—so that you feel confident that your entries will remain private. If you haven't already begun the habit, start collecting pictures or images from magazines, the greeting cards you just couldn't throw out, newspaper ads, pictures from last year's calendar, poems, and old letters. These are the ideas and images that speak to your soul without you necessarily knowing why: they are the tools that will take you on journeys into other parts of yourself, past and future.

Six Months to Live

Imagine that you have just learned that you have only six more months to live. Write for fifteen minutes on how you would respond to the news. Are there aspects of your daily life that you would change? Would you nurture yourself differently? Would you make any changes in your relationship with your child? With your partner? As you review your life, what causes you regret and what brings satisfaction? Are there ways to incorporate these insights into your life now?

Saving Face

Spend some time looking through magazines and ads for an image of a woman five to ten years older than you. She needn't be famous, but if she is, be sure that what you're seeing is the real thing, unaltered by plastic surgery or computer science. You might need to seek out magazines that cater to special interests, like art, psychology, archaeology, or science, where women actually *do* things and are engaged in interesting lives. When you find a face that has a quality that moves you, cut it out and paste it in your Journey Book.

Look at the image you've put in your book and write about what you see in her face that inspires you. Maybe it's how the wrinkles let you know she laughs a lot, or how she is not ashamed to show her sorrow. Write about what you've seen in your own face that reveals the truth about you.

Leave plenty of blank pages for this exercise and come back to it whenever you need to process your feelings about aging in a youth-worshiping culture. Over time it has been my experience that this exercise leads subtly toward a gradual acceptance and affirmation of the potential beauty inherent in aging. It also opens us up to the possibility of meeting what the Buddhists call our "Original Face," the one that lives behind the mask. Reassured that we do not have to depend on our bodies for our worth, we are free to redefine beauty and show a truer face to the world.

WE HAVE THE POWER

In your Journey Book, write prose, make a collage with photos or images, or make a list that declares your power, vision, and unique gifts. What talents and skills do you intuitively know you are developing as an older woman but are hesitant to acknowledge? How might you share them—with your child, your partner, your community, society as a whole? Do you know other women who might share in your growing sense of empowerment? Is there the potential for a collective vision or collective action?

Write about the power that is yours to be claimed. This is the power that has the ability to nurture the sacred spiritual life of a family and a community, and that has led other cultures into periods of great prosperity and peace. Know that this is your birthright *because* of your age, not *despite* it.

CHAPTER TWO

The Clash of the Titans:
Motherhood Meets Menopause

By the time I hit forty, my friends had put me into the
category of someone who could cope with anything. But
now I've got night sweats, mood swings, my energy level
is dropping, and I'm a single mother with a six-year-old
daughter. It took me awhile to admit that I'm in a whole
new category.

BELLA, FORTY-SIX-YEAR-OLD MOTHER OF SIX-YEAR-OLD ZOE

Motherhood and menopause are considered two distinct
phases of a woman's reproductive life cycle. But what if they
happen just years apart? What if the activities and sacrifices
appropriate to motherhood—giving selflessly to a child any
time of the day or well into the night, postponing short-term
pleasures and long-term goals for the good of the family—are
at odds with the impulses that rise up inside the midlife
woman—the physical call to slow down, the desire to ingather
and reflect on the second half of her life, the hunger to put
her own needs first? What happens when these two sets of
developmentally appropriate needs collide? I call this the
"Clash of the Titans," the detonation that sounds inside the

older woman who is caught between responding to her own mounting needs and to those of her young child.

A woman who has postponed motherhood until her forties looks forward to showering her child with all the unconditional love that she has been saving up for decades. Unfortunately, she may not have factored the following into her biological timetable: as a woman in her forties, she is more than likely entering perimenopause. This means that, although she is still menstruating, her hormones have probably begun to fluctuate as they did during the wild ride of puberty.

We roll our eyes when we talk about self-centered teenagers. "Hormones," we say, to explain their often unexplainable erratic emotional behavior. They forget to feed the dog. They space out when you talk to them. They spend hours in their room alone or on the phone with a friend. This self-absorption seems to come with the teenage turf.

Midlife presents the older woman with the same hormonally predisposed imperative to turn inward and focus on herself. It's a time to take stock of how she has lived the first half of her life. With whom has she shared her time, her love, her money, and her energy? Has she followed her dreams and passions? Has she contributed to the community? When midlife women look in the mirror and know for sure that youth is fading and aging is inevitable, many of them seize the opportunity to make big changes as they head into the second half of their lives. They go back to school, get married or divorced, start the business they put on hold twenty years ago, sell it all and go traveling, or retreat to a monastery. Many of these women say they feel like they are becoming outrageous, like the lid is coming off and they can't control what they say anymore. All that has been repressed steps forward, right smack into the middle of their personalities. If they were "good girls," the midlife woman from hell is about to step from behind the curtain and yell, "BOO!"

Perimenopausal women make up the group that most often reports fatigue, wild mood swings, and mental instability to their doctors. Unfortunately, many of these doctors over-prescribe antidepressants, which can be as great a disservice to the woman poised on the threshold of the second half of her life as it would be to the teenager struggling to find her emotional and mental balance on the brink of adulthood. This same woman will eventually ride out the hormonal storm and find her footing, mentally, physically, and emotionally, but if it will be years before her child is grown, she may find herself wondering if she'll have enough energy left to pursue her own dreams.

> My daughter is going through puberty at the same time I'm going through menopause. It's hard to tell which one of us is more hormonally crazed.
>
> SUSAN, FIFTY-TWO-YEAR-OLD MOTHER OF TWELVE-YEAR-OLD EDEN

This is the essence of the conflict many women bring to my First-Time Moms over Forty support groups. They ask: "How can I reconcile the time I need for myself with the endless responsibilities (and joys) of motherhood?"

Up until now, older first-time mothers have been offered little guidance in resolving this clash of needs and were left feeling guilty, confused, and privately ashamed. This chapter is designed to help you successfully resolve this conflict. There is nothing more reassuring than hearing the voices of other older mothers who, like you, adore their children at the same time they struggle to honor their own midlife imperatives. The suggestions are specifically geared toward helping you claim guilt-free time for yourself by learning to identify and accept your ambivalence, setting healthy limits, scaling back expectations as a way of coping with fatigue, and putting yourself on the list of people you regularly nurture. These suggestions never assume that you have more time for yourself than you really do, nor do they underestimate how daunting the clash of needs can be. Like the emergency instructions on an airplane, you'll be shown how to secure your own oxygen mask first, so that you'll then be able to help those who need your time, attention, patience, and love.

Accepting Your Ambivalence

Many of the first-time older mothers I work with have a hard time admitting that they have feelings of ambivalence. Ambivalence simply means having mutually conflicting emotions, but in our linear society, it's hard to understand that we can hold two seemingly disparate feelings at the same time. For instance, we love being a mother and miss our children after a two-hour separation, but we also remember our single days with longing. We adore the security and warmth of our family, even as we dream of taking refuge in a Buddhist monastery. Mothers who know that this will most likely be their only child not only feel required to "do it all," but also to be unambivalently enthusiastic while they're doing it. Doris, a forty-nine-year-old teacher who dotes on her nine-year-old daughter, wonders, "Am I the only one who wishes my child would dematerialize, get beamed up and away for the day, and return ready for bed?" Sherry,

At forty-two, with a two-year-old, I was overloaded, angry, and losing it. I went to three female doctors who all told me that menopause couldn't be happening because I was still getting my period. Maybe they thought you had to be fifty and you had to have stopped your period. I finally found a doctor who thought I was perimenopausal. What made me really want to deal with it was not wanting my daughter to grow up thinking I was just a crazy old lady. What kind of role model would that be for her?

VIRGINIA, FIFTY-FIVE-YEAR-OLD MOTHER OF FIFTEEN-YEAR-OLD FELICIA a forty-seven-year-old woman devoted to her two-year-old son, confides to our support group that she has fantasies of buying a red Harley and disappearing into a "witness protection program for older mothers."

Does this ambivalence mean these women don't love their children? Not at all. It means that after decades of cherished autonomy and independence, first-time older mothers find their previous lifestyle and all its freedoms altered beyond recognition. It means that this surrender of self-rule comes at precisely the time most midlife women with grown children are just beginning to reclaim their lives. To acknowledge the inevitable ambivalence that arises when the demands of putting another person's needs first clash with the midlife call toward selfhood is not an admission of failure. It simply means you are human and are feeling more than one thing at the same time.

Suzanne, a forty-nine-year-old business administrator and mother of eight-year-old Sara, had the support group groaning and laughing as she described what happened the day before she was about to leave on a much-needed two-day weekend retreat by herself.

"Sara wanted to know why she couldn't come with me," she said, "so I had to explain about how I needed to take some time away for myself. But still, I was feeling pretty conflicted about it. So by the time she asked me to take her to the Laundromat to help her wash her giant quilt, I said yes. It had been an intense day at work and I was feeling pretty hormonal. I probably should have known better, but my guilt got the better of

> Diet, exercise, rest, meditation, gardening, dancing, writing, whatever centers you. Self-care is a critical factor for an older mom. It's so easy to put yourself on the back burner. You eat last if at all, you exercise if you can fit it in, you sleep when you can. There has to be a real conscious effort to take care of yourself, because if you don't juice yourself up, your child is going to suffer.
>
> DEBRA, FORTY-THREE-YEAR-OLD MOM OF THREE-YEAR-OLD TYLER

me. After two hours of sitting in this smelly Laundromat, watching really bad TV, with the bathroom out of order, she drags the damn quilt through an oil spill on the way to the car. I totally lost it and began haranguing her about how she needed to focus more. So then I got into the car and I proceeded to back up over one of those concrete row dividers they have in parking lots. Men came out of the Laundromat to watch me. Blessedly my daughter didn't say a word on the way home. But while we were eating dinner my husband asked us how the day had gone, and of course she told him everything—how I had given her a 'big old lecture on being focused' while I was backing up over this thing, and how half the town had come out to watch me. So my husband put his fork down and said to her, 'Honey, that's why Mommy needs to go away.'"

Anna told the support group she felt devastated because, after spending thousands of dollars and three years undergoing infertility treatments, she was now feeling increasingly frustrated and impatient with her four-year-old daughter. "I'm forty-seven," she began. "My periods are irregular, and sometimes I feel so hormonally out of balance and so desperate for time alone that I lock myself in the bathroom. Last week I yelled so loud my daughter burst into tears and said, 'I want my *real* mommy.' How could this possibly be me, the same woman who tried to have a baby for so many years? Sometimes I say I'm going to the store, but really all I do is just sit in the car in the parking lot soaking up the silence, knowing no one can find me and ask me for anything. My husband knows I need time to be alone and encourages me to take it, but I'm torn. I'm not going to have any more children, and if I leave, I might miss something precious. But when I stay, I'm

> Paradoxical as it may seem, to believe in youth is to look backward; to look forward we must believe in age.
>
> Dorothy Parker

38

crabby and I want to escape. I guess you could say I'm caught between a rock and a hard place."

These women are incredibly relieved when they understand that this powerful urge to claim time and space for themselves is an inherent component of the midlife passage. Taking this time away allows them to return to their families recharged and rebalanced. But if this impulse is ignored or condemned, they stay caught in unresolved ambivalence, often growing irritable and depressed, and end up alienated from the ones they love the very most.

Learning to Set Limits

A number of older moms who come to my support groups often tell me that one of their greatest difficulties is learning to say no to their children when their thoughts, feelings, and body cues are telling them that they are too overwhelmed to say yes. Yet significantly the one regret that older parents with grown children consistently express is a wish that they had set more limits with their children early on. So what is it that prevents us from drawing a line in the sand and establishing these much-needed limits with our children?

I felt like huge pieces of my old self were being vacuumed up in being a parent until I arranged my schedule to be home alone once a week. I put fresh flowers on the table, turn off the phone, and take a hot bath. I make a point not to accomplish a single, tangible thing.

JESSE, FORTY-FIVE-YEAR-OLD MOTHER OF FIVE-YEAR-OLD KYLE

For many midlife moms, the difficulty arises because they know they are only going to have one child, and they can't bear being too strict. Other women say that they hold themselves to unrealistic expectations of perfect parenting, which includes never having to say no. Those who came of age in an era that encouraged breaking free of limitations now equate limit setting with restricting their child's developing

39

self-esteem. It's also common for older parents of only children to relate to their children as friends because they spend so much time together, but it then becomes that much harder to switch into the role of boundary setter.

Most of us truly enjoy the pleasure of caring for our children, but if we judge ourselves when we attempt to establish boundaries, we may be resurrecting old beliefs about setting limits that have slipped into our unconscious and now influence our behavior. "A loving mother always puts the needs of her child first. If she doesn't, she's selfish" is a common misperception. Or, "I'm no better than my mother was. She was always off somewhere when I needed her." Another thought that can stop us in our tracks is, "If I go off and take time for myself, something horrible will happen to my child." While most mothers logically know that they'll be better parents if they take care of themselves, these beliefs have had decades to solidify and can prevent us from meeting our own needs.

Julie found it particularly difficult to set limits because, after years of waiting to have a baby, she had enormous expectations of herself and a hidden belief that prioritizing her own needs made her a negligent mother. "For all my years of growth and success at becoming a better person, once I had Katie I began to feel like I was unraveling. I couldn't find my center. I had been in recovery for thirteen years before I had her at forty-three. I waited because I wanted to make sure there was enough love inside me to go around. Before I had her, I used to devote a big chunk of my day to yoga and meditation and running. Now I have to squeeze all of that into fifteen minutes. Everyone tells me to put her in day care now that she's three, but I can't do it. This is my only chance to be a mom. But still, I push myself past the point where it's healthy to be with her. Sometimes I've had enough after twenty minutes, and I really want to go take some quiet time, but I continue playing with her for another hour. Then I find myself yelling at her and being a really uptight mom. It makes me feel so bad. I don't know why I wait so long to take time for myself. One time I let her come into my room when I did yoga, but she was too young to understand, and she kept crawling under my legs. I blew it and yelled and then felt so bad that I didn't even try to do yoga again for months. But the thing is, when I do finally take time for myself, I come back filled up and nothing bad has happened to her. I expect myself to be Mother Teresa, patient and wise, but she spends hours a day in prayer and meditation and I don't even give myself twenty minutes to recharge."

Every five minutes I spend setting consistent limits with my child saves me fifteen minutes of turmoil.

ELLA, FORTY-FOUR-YEAR-OLD MOTHER OF THREE-YEAR-OLD NATASHA

This reluctance to set limits and claim time for herself, as well as the ensuing negotiations and constant infringements on the time she has set aside, can be one of the most fundamental causes of an older mother's short fuse. "Mommy, are you mad at me? Are you okay?" four-year-old Allison asks Rae, her forty-four-year-old mother who has withdrawn behind closed doors for five minutes of recharging. "I don't want her to think I'm angry, so I let her come in, and then we do whatever she wants to do," Rae told me. "I've never said, 'No, you can't come in. I need to be by myself now.' It's getting harder and harder for me to take any time alone now. She can talk me into anything."

Your child will test your limits, and it's developmentally appropriate for them to do so. But we are doing them a great disservice if we give them the impression that they never have to learn how to manage the disappointment of not always getting their wishes granted. While we may be afraid that setting limits jeopardizes the relationship, in fact, kids feel loved and

41

thrive with the security and safety this kind of structure provides. Clear-cut, well-established limits also provide the means by which we can meet our own needs without having to resort to erratic, unpredictable behavior. When the time is right and the emotional waters in the household are calm, sit down with your family and establish the fact that there are going to be times of the day or night when mommy takes time for herself.

Feeling selfish when we prioritize ourselves above someone else is a gene defect, and most women have it.

DONNA, FORTY-NINE-YEAR-OLD MOTHER OF SIX-YEAR-OLD SAM

Instead of a child thinking that she must have done something wrong for mommy to go away behind a closed door, he or she can begin seeing this as normal, predictable behavior. Life begins to feel safe again for a child who may have been frightened by mom's shifting moods. By normalizing the need to take time away, children come to expect that mommy will not always be available and that it's not their fault. One creative mother I know utilized an "Off-Limits, Quiet Time" sign on her door, which she and her eight-year-old daughter made together. It was so appealing to her daughter that she asked if she could have one for her room too.

I encourage older women to create a parenting style that builds in adult time and interests from the beginning, whether that time is made possible by day care, paid help, or trading with other parents, family, or friends. Kids adapt well to clear messages. If the message is that mom loves you a lot, and mom also has a life of her own, beyond work, that needs tending, they'll do fine. A major part of the developmental task for a child is learning to live with a certain amount of distress when they don't always get their own way. And part of the developmental task of loving parents is to discern that this distress is not only not life-threatening, it is essential to the emotional well-being and growth of their child.

The Body Knows

After several years of parenting, most of us know what to expect when we don't set limits with our children. We lose our patience and yell, we feel resentful and frustrated, and then we're overcome with remorse. Here's a technique I have found that allows your body to tell you when you are about to say yes when you really mean no, when you are about to go over the top of what you genuinely have to give, when you need to stop and set a limit. I have a small muscle in my right shoulder that twitches madly when I am dangerously close to denying my own pressing needs in favor of someone else's. I've come to think of it like Jimminy Cricket desperate to get Pinocchio's attention. It's my own personal warning signal. If I don't set a limit now, I'm heading over the cliff into an emotional danger zone. When I pay attention, I pull back just in the nick of time, and the reward is acting like the loving human being I know I can be. When I establish and respect my limits in an interaction with my daughter, I feel like a virtuous June Cleaver for the rest of the day. When I ignore my internal radar, I end up yelling in order to get my needs met. Afterward, I slink around feeling like Mommy Dearest. Once the mothers in my support groups begin to listen to their body cues, they report telltale twitching eyelids, tight stomachs, and sweaty palms. Learning to interpret these messages from your body will mean you have a choice in the cool of the moment to set a healthy limit and stop short of having to blow a fuse in order to get your own needs met.

Authority versus Abuse

For some of the older mothers I counsel, a reluctance to set limits is even more pronounced if they were emotionally or sexually abused as children. Their difficulty acknowledging and establishing legitimate limits stems from confusion around the difference between authority and abuse. They vowed that when they became parents, they would make life perfect for their children, free from the suffering they endured. Now they fear that asserting their parental authority is perpetrating a form of abuse. They shrink from setting limits with their children for fear that they will harm them. If you are having difficulty distinguishing between the healthy authority you need to assume as a parent and the abuse from your past, I encourage you to seek out the professional help of a therapist or counselor. Working through this issue will enable you to become a more effective parent as well as a more fulfilled individual.

> To love without role, without power plays, is revolution.
>
> RITA MAE BROWN

Coping with Fatigue by Scaling Back Expectations

While all mothers feel tired, the perimenopausal mother's fatigue is compounded by her post-birth/premenopausal hormone cocktail. This potent mix creates a bone-deep fatigue that is poignantly juxtaposed against the high-energy needs of her young child. These women felt young and vital before they had their babies. Now it's common to hear them say, "I can't believe how tired I am most of the time." One mother lamented, "I'm always too tired to play with my daughter. I can just hear her talking about it in therapy twenty years from now." Another added, "Now I drool thinking about sleep the way I used to thinking about sex."

In group sessions, when I mention the memory lapses, fuzzy thinking, and lack of concentration associated with midlife fatigue, I can count on hilarity in seconds: "I found the missing scissors in the refrigerator. Did I do that? That's it, I thought. I've got a brain tumor." "I couldn't remember my best friend's last name. Hell, I can barely remember my own last name!" "My daughter and I went to a spring equinox ritual. Everyone had to bring a slip of paper with their wishes for themselves and their families written on it. We put them all in a bowl and burned them in a very beautiful ceremony. The next day I found my wish list in my pocket. I must have burned my shopping list."

Not only is there a biochemical component to the fatigue at midlife, there is the additional exponential factor that comes from always being on call. You can't follow the body's imperative to rest if it's time to pick your child up from school or cook dinner. Successfully devising strategies to cope with this level of fatigue may mean scaling back on your expectations of yourself, and often it involves seismic shifts in self-image.

Carmine was a high-powered computer programmer before she had her daughter three years ago. Now at forty-five, she's creating a new lifestyle that includes concessions to a fatigue that she admits "caught me by surprise. I used to be a career woman—panty hose, high heels, the whole scene. After my daughter was born, I switched to part time, and then to running my own consulting business from home. At first, I got dressed up every day like I did when I worked in the city. Then I just admitted to myself that I was pooped and switched to wearing sweats. I had "day sweats" to work in and "night sweats" to sleep in. But one day I came out of my office around lunchtime and my daughter asked me if I was going to work or to bed. Believe me, it was a shock to see how far I'd come from my power suit days."

> I was breastfeeding at forty-seven, the same year my periods began getting irregular. When my thinking got a bit fuzzy, I chalked it up to my menopausal lactation brain.
>
> CARLA, FORTY-NINE-YEAR-OLD MOTHER OF THREE-YEAR-OLD CATHERINE

Laura, a forty-five-year-old client of mine, has been a successful commercial artist for twenty years. She had her first and only child five years ago and has been juggling motherhood, marriage, and career ever since. "I don't have the reserves of energy I used to have," she told me. "I used to pride myself on my gourmet cooking, but now, if I'm involved in a painting, and it's dinnertime, I don't stop to cook. I know I'm fooling myself if I think I'll have the energy to cook *and* get back to work later. I probably would have been pulled in more directions if I were younger. Now I want time for my family and my art. These matter. We can always order take-out."

The Luscious Horizontal Position (but Not What You Think)

Feeling too tired and spaced out to play with your child can be a great disappointment not only to your child but also to yourself. Fortunately, children care more about you being with them than they do about whether you're sitting up or lying down, so at the end of the day I recommend scaling back your expectations and playing "lying down" games. You and your child can read together, play cards together, watch movies together. Despite the fact that I always thought I would outlaw videos in favor of more "creative" endeavors and certainly thought I would be more physically active when I became a parent, some of my most treasured memories come from the humor my daughter and I have shared watching cartoons and movies together, all from a luscious horizontal position.

The Party from Hell

I wish I always followed my own good advice. Last week was my daughter's twelfth birthday, and she wanted a mammoth Romanesque celebration: a trip to the amusement park with four of her best friends; a dinner party for eight with all of her favorite foods; an elaborate birthday cake, ice cream, and helium balloons; and a sleepover in her tree house. Now it may be easy for you to say *no way,* but I got caught up in my desire to grant her every wish. Against my better judgment, I created this three-ring circus and then paid dearly for it. These preteen girls were so hormonally wound up and so overstimulated that they climbed up and down the tree house ladder giggling, whispering, and needing flashlights, snacks, and comfort well into the night. The next day I looked at my bedraggled self in the mirror and thought about the expectations that had created the Birthday Party from Hell for the introverted older mother that I am. Next year, when that lying, thieving little birthday fairy whispers in my ear, "Go on, you can do it . . . give her everything she wants," I'll have my wits about me and be lying in wait.

I used to make elaborate custard pies when I went to a potluck. Now when I think of the time it will take to buy the ingredients, do the cooking and the clean-up—all precious time when my son is in school—I think I'd rather spend the time taking care of myself and bring pies from the local health food store. Frankly no one really cares what kind of pies I bring, but if they did, I'd say, "What you think of me is none of my business."

KIMBERLY, FORTY-FIVE-YEAR-OLD MOTHER OF FOUR-YEAR-OLD BEN

Fighting Fatigue with Better Nutrition

If you are among the many first-time moms over forty who are experiencing the fatigue or mild depression associated with perimenopause, never underestimate the positive effect that increasing your vitamin and mineral intake can have on your energy level and your moods. Go to your local bookstore or library and check out the many good books available that detail the changing nutritional needs of the perimenopausal woman. I have worked with many mothers who thought they were candidates not only for the old folk's farm but for antidepressants as well. Many of these women responded successfully to boosting their vitamin and mineral intake. Some of my clients also report increased energy and a brighter mental outlook from acupuncture and Chinese herbs. And if you don't already do some form of regular exercise as a means of boosting your energy, refer to chapter one for painless, pleasurable guidelines.

If you suspect that part of your fatigue is due to your hormones fluctuating and you want to find out the specifics, I recommend that instead of relying on traditional blood tests, which are not highly sensitive to subtle shifts in hormonal levels, you seek out a health care practitioner who offers the more advanced saliva sample method. See Resources (page 196) for more information on how to find a hormone testing service.

Putting Yourself on the List

In your quest to maintain a career, a relationship, and a dust-bunny-free home, and to meet your child's needs plus still have time left over for romantic interludes with your partner, the needs you most likely are not tending to are your own. This is all the more poignant because as older first-time moms, we have had years to grow into the individuals we are today and probably can remember lots of ways we used to restore and nurture ourselves B.C.—Before Children. One forty-six-year-old client told me, "The realization hit me on about day seven after my son was born that my life was over as I had known it. My routines, my private time, my time for journaling, thinking, writing, painting, it was all just gone."

To make matters worse, most of the popular books written for midlife women that encourage them to use these years as an opportunity for personal transformation and creative exploration are clearly not written for women with young children. One woman told the group, "My friend sent me this really great book that recommended that women going through menopause spend three days every full moon and three days every new moon retreating by herself to gather power. I put the book down and took stock of my life. I *used* to do things like that all the time. Now it was three o'clock in the afternoon. I was at home with a kid who was either playing Legos or jumping off the sofa in a Batman costume. I was about to start dinner. Then I'd do the dishes, give him a bath, read a story, and tuck him in. It would be 9:30 before I had a moment to myself again. 'Get real!' I wanted to shout at the book. I'd be lucky to get my teeth brushed, let alone six days a month to myself."

These losses are real. Midlife motherhood has granted us our most heartfelt wish, while it has taken from us cherished parts of our youth and freedom. I fervently believe from my experience working with older first-time moms that by remembering, honoring, and *incorporating* parts of ourselves that thrived before we became parents, we can stay sane, balanced, and recharged. It's like swimming upstream, back to your place of origin.

Before I got my hormones tested and knew which supplements to take, my mood swings were very erratic. I felt irritable and fragile, like I was inside an egg about to break. To be hormonally depleted as an older mother of a young child is a real double whammy. Now I feel like I can hold my life together.

MARLA, FORTY-EIGHT-YEAR-OLD MOTHER OF FOUR-YEAR-OLD JUSTINE

I was reminded of this several months ago when I went for a walk and ended up in my neighborhood park, where a primitive but beautiful labyrinth had recently been created out of our indigenous adobe soil. Impulsively, I walked through the archway and began circling my way through the maze. When I got to the center, I sat on the stone bench and for the first time that day appreciated the breathtaking New Mexico morning. High puffy clouds hung in a bright blue sky, red-winged blackbirds called to each other from crab apple trees bursting with bloom. For a moment I was transported back to my years as a single woman when I took delight in traveling alone to foreign countries. I loved going without companions because it left me free to follow the spontaneous call of adventure. Walking through that arch and following my impulse to sit on that stone instantly recalled the woman I had been before my career, my marriage, and my family. Before pets and gardens. Before taxes and PTA meetings. Before I had a clue what havoc midlife hormonal changes could wreak. I knew I didn't want to *be* her again, I just wished I could *visit* with her more often.

I (she) had a great fondness for watching a sunrise from a hilltop, but—I'm sure this will come as no surprise—I have only managed that feat once during the last five years. Other pleasures I (she) enjoyed that I indulge in more frequently include going out to breakfast alone, rummaging through flea markets, foraging for wild medicinal herbs, spending luxurious time on the telephone gossiping with my best friend, getting a massage from a woman with strong hands and a kind heart, buying too many platform shoes, and going to a 1:30 matinee. I have a girlfriend who puts on a nostalgic old pair of cowboy boots and goes dancing every time she feels like life has nailed her to the ground.

Sit quietly and remember the life you led before you became a mother. Remember the ways you had of taking care of yourself. Let your mind run wild and imagine how you might incorporate some of this good medicine into your life now, each day or each week. It doesn't matter if you're inclined to gather and drink wild herbs, or meet a friend for a shot of scotch, straight up. Personally I've done both. What matters is that you take the time to care for yourself. And while I believe there is a special hell reserved for those who urge hormonally challenged and physically depleted midlife mothers to "just do it," there are instantaneous and life-affirming benefits to putting yourself on the list of the people you regularly nurture.

Seek out and connect with other older first-time moms like yourself. Put up notices on bulletin boards or in local classifieds. You'll find sample ads and an eight-week curriculum in the appendix (page 183). When appropriate, help each other with childcare and housecleaning so that each of you gets what you need—precious time to be with yourself and with others so that you can return to parenting renewed and inspired.

Individually and collectively we've pushed the envelope and extended the time line for fertility. First-time mothers over forty are a rapidly growing demographic—fast becoming commonplace rather than exceptional. We've proven that we can have healthy beautiful babies well into our forties. Now the challenge is to draw new maps for the next generation of older first-time moms, illuminating the territory where the needs of the midlife mother and her child can meet.

The Journey Book

SETTING LIMITS

When you have the time, sit quietly with your Journey Book. Think of five situations in which you would like to set clearer limits. Write them down.

Are there any beliefs or judgments you hold that may be preventing you from setting these limits?

Reflect on what happens when you say yes when you really need to say no. Write for five minutes, stream of consciousness, the completion of the following sentence: "I know I've neglected my own needs for too long when I. . . ."

EMBRACING YOUR AMBIVALENCE

The following exercise has proven highly effective for the women in my support groups who are grappling with issues of ambivalence. It is designed to help you get comfortable with the fact that there are several voices inside of you that are clamoring for equal airtime. Some of these voices are ones with whom you are familiar. Others may be ones you are repressing because of the pressures and responsibilities of motherhood. All of them need to be heard and accepted if you hope to successfully reconcile your dual identities of individual and mother.

Pick two of the distinct parts of you that are seeking res-olution and reconciliation. Wild woman and devoted mother? Solitary world traveler and neighborhood carpooler? Now imagine that each one of these characters has come alive and has invited you into her home. Visit with each one separately. Write a description of each character and note the specifics of each personality. What are they wearing? Is one dressed in lace and a low-cut dress and the other in jeans? Does one plan for the future and one live in the moment? Is one's refrig-erator empty except for wine and cheese? What do they do for entertainment? Work? Are they married or single? What kind of music do they listen to, and who are their friends? What would the ideal vacation be for each of them? How do they prefer to spend their time? Give your imagination free rein as you flesh out the various tastes, styles, and, most important, needs that are coexisting inside of you. It is a safe first step toward embracing your ambivalence without judgment or cen-sorship, and restoring those parts of yourself that may have been suppressed, denied, or forbidden. (Thanks to Deena Metzger and her wonderful book *Writing for Your Life* for the inspiration for this exercise.)

Putting Yourself on the List

There *was* a you before motherhood. Make a list or create a collage that reflects who you were and what you liked to do before you became a parent. List five creative ways to make contact with this other you at least once a week.

CHAPTER THREE

Honoring Our Choices:
Balancing Work and Motherhood

I would have resented my kids if I had had them any younger. My friends are very surprised that I am a good mother because I was so driven and career oriented. But being older is helpful because I can see what I have to do to keep everything in balance. When I work, I'm at work. When I come home, I'm a mom. I do a lot for myself. I have lunch with my friends, I exercise, I garden. I just want to make what I have work well for all of us. I don't need to be a Superwoman.

CECILIA, FORTY-FOUR-YEAR-OLD MOTHER
OF THREE-YEAR-OLD CARL

One of the most significant changes that has occurred in our society over the last forty years has been the dramatic increase in the number of women in the workforce. Sixty percent of the 105 million women in the United States over the age of sixteen have paid jobs, and 46.2 percent of all workers are women; by 2005 this percentage of women in the labor force is projected to rise to 61.7 percent. Fewer than 20 percent of married-couple households still follow the traditional male breadwinner/female homemaker model, and there is a growing number of working families headed by single mothers as well as two-income families made up of lesbian or gay couples and their children. Despite the dramatic changes in the role of middle-class women as mother and worker (and despite the challenge of meeting the ever-rising cost of living), public solutions to the personal dilemma of balancing family and work, such as family-friendly workplace policies and universal childcare, are still for the most part extremely limited or unavailable.

For the fortysomething first-time mother, balancing work life and home life becomes even more complex. If she has cultivated a career for fifteen or twenty years, her career is likely to be at that place in its trajectory where it is just about to soar. "Sequencing"—the popular notion advocating that mothers take a three- or four-year hiatus from work after the birth of their child to be a stay-at-home mom, and then reenter the workforce—is not an option. She is likely to jeopardize promotions, salary advances, peer recognition, and retirement benefits, and there are not enough work years left at this point in her career to risk losing touch with the advances in her field. "And besides," as one client put it, "I'd be a forty-seven-year-old dinosaur when I came back, and who'd want to hire me?"

Some midlife mothers who can afford it financially take a "been there/done that, I've proved myself in the world" attitude. They trade in work advancement for the pleasure of staying home with their child and enjoy what they see as their only chance at motherhood. These women consistently report grappling with their loss of earning power and prestige out in the world, and a diminished sense of equality with their partners. Other mothers piece together a lifestyle alone or with their partners that accommodates parental responsibilities and scaled-back work hours; they know that maintaining a part-time work life outside of and apart from motherhood is essential to their well-being and sanity.

Perhaps it's our grass-is-always-greener mentality that lends weight to the notion that any of these choices is stress-free. They're not. They all have their demands and limitations, and they all involve some degree of loss, whether that loss is income and prestige or having someone else see your child's first steps. Trying to determine which choice is "better" from the perspective of the child's well-being is faulty at best. The conventional wisdom that labeled working mothers neglectful and their children damaged has been proven untrue. Recent studies have repeatedly found that when mothers are doing what they feel is right for themselves and their families and feel satisfied with their roles—whether it's working full or part time or not working at all—their children are likely to prosper. Having a mom who feels satisfied not stressed, supported not overwhelmed, at work *or* at home, is what matters most to children. When we can honor our choices, whether it's working outside the home or working inside the home, because we know that "ain't nobody happy if mama not happy," we can begin to reconcile our ambivalence and losses within the context of making decisions that are ultimately the most rewarding for us.

Just as our needs change with age, our children's do too. They grow and pass through developmental stages in which they want and need to spend more or less time with us, and it's a never-ending juggling act to accommodate them. The childcare arrangements that work when a child is an infant no longer apply when she enters preschool. The three-year-old who was content to stay at preschool until five o'clock has grown into a seven-year-old who has a heartfelt need to be picked up from elementary school at three. Weighing the needs

of our family within the context of honoring our own fulfillment is an enormous challenge, especially in our society, which
still relegates the issue of how to successfully raise the next
generation to the Lifestyle section of the Sunday paper. Without the benefit of cultural precedent, first-time mothers over
forty are making individual career choices based on what works
within their own families, and then finding ways to create the
support they need to maintain this precarious balance.

Continuing Your Career

Many of the women who work strictly out of financial necessity say that if they had enough money, they would quit in a
heartbeat. But for some midlife mothers, their work is not only
a source of income but identity, self-esteem, and fulfillment as
well. Having a child and continuing to cultivate their career at
this stage of life means making strategic decisions about where
to invest time and energy, and how to reconcile the inevitable
losses that come from these hard choices.

I got a call one day from my old friend Jayne, who asked
if we could meet for lunch at a Chinese restaurant. A forty-
seven-year-old archeologist and the author of several highly
regarded books in her field, Jayne went back to graduate
school in her late twenties after the end of her first marriage
and spent the next seven years earning her Ph.D. Once she
began to work, she flourished in a world of rich intellectual
stimulation and well-earned financial rewards. She married her
current husband, also an archeologist, when she was thirty-
nine and gave birth to their daughter, Ariel, when she was a
few months shy of forty-one. She resumed work six months
later, confident in the childcare she had arranged for her
daughter. Now six years later, Jayne wanted to talk about the

growing complexity of maintaining her career and meeting the changing needs of her child.

"The biological imperative hit me hard, and having Ariel was the most important thing to me," she said. "I wasn't necessarily thinking about how having a child was going to impact my career or my time. But having a baby in childcare is really different than having a six-year-old who wants to be home more. My daughter is either in school or in aftercare ten hours a day, and she doesn't like it at all. There are just too many people with too many sets of rules caring for her.

"I can't leave my work now," Jayne continued. "Maybe if I had had her when I was thirty I could stay home for the next few years and then get back on my feet professionally, but there isn't that much time left in my work future. Even being away from the field for two years is too long. I'd never catch up with all the advances in theory being made.

"I've had forty years of doing things that were important only to me, and honestly," she said, "it's hard to get out of that habit. Now I'm at a midlife crossroads trying to figure out what I'm going to sacrifice. Can I accomplish my career goals in the time I have left, and is that more important than my daughter being away from me ten hours a day? Maybe if Ariel were older I'd have the luxury of working without conflict because her needs wouldn't be so much of a determining factor in what I'm going to do with the next ten years of my life."

My mother never thought about herself. She always got the burnt toast. But when the kids went out the door for school she had the whole day ahead of her to do the chores—the stuff I do on weekends. In a way, she was able to take care of herself because there were times of the day that she had for herself. She'd do the errands by herself, she'd go off to play bridge and spend some time with her friends. Even though what she was doing was taking care of the family during most of that time, she wasn't having to continuously be interacting with the family. She *could* be the last person served because there was time for her during the day.

KELLY, FORTY-SEVEN-YEAR-OLD MOTHER OF SIX-YEAR-OLD LUKE

Jayne sometimes looks around at the women in her field who decided not to have children and envies their lack of conflict, "but you have to put things in perspective," she said. "Mostly I see them missing out. Ariel has enriched my life in so many ways. She's restored my delight in Christmas, and all the things I had grown tired of, like camping, are new to me now through her eyes."

While Jayne knows that her daughter would prefer to have a mommy that doesn't go to work, she hopes that because working is good for *her* mentally and emotionally, it will ultimately be good for the family as a whole. Jayne and her husband share a long-range plan for the family that includes "an incredibly attractive retirement package that we'll be eligible for in ten years. It will provide for Ariel's college," she said. "We'd be crazy to give that up now."

Our meal was over and the waiter brought us our fortune cookies. Jayne seemed amused with hers: "You show great administrative skills." "It's true that I won't be a stay-at-home mom when she's six," she said, "but when I retire she'll be sixteen, and maybe that's when she'll *really* need me to be around."

Jayne's decision to continue her career was based on a realistic assessment of her need for intellectual fulfillment and a secure financial retirement. She understands that meeting these goals might mean not being available for her daughter after school, but she's learning to live without the impossible expectation that she "should" be able to do it all. Lately she's begun to think of herself as a role model for her daughter—a loving parent engaged in the world—rather than someone with a problem that needs correcting.

If we can acknowledge from the outset that pursuing a meaningful career as a midlife mother means facing some inevitable losses, we can involve our families in defining what really matters to each of us and make strategic choices with wisdom and forethought. "My son is really into soccer," one full-time career mama of forty-eight with an eight-year-old child told me. "I come home late most days and miss all of his practices, so I promised him that I'd arrange my schedule to be there for his games. Now it's like a mission statement I've written for myself. If I get into a work situation where I begin to rationalize being too busy to go to his games, I can self-correct right away."

Performances, birthdays, games—these are some of the events at which you can guarantee your presence will matter to your child. The list changes with each family. Some kids don't want anyone but their mom taking them to a doctor's appointment and only dad will do when it comes to driving lessons. Working out what matters most to you and your family and then creating a personal "mission statement" becomes one way to assess whether or not you're maintaining your balance at work and within your family system. These become the nonnegotiable milestones that you make every effort humanly possible to honor. Instead of feeling overwhelmed by an amorphous list of all the things you *can't* do and *should* be doing, honestly acknowledging limitations and priorities becomes a creative opportunity for everyone to have a say in the shaping of their lives.

Scaling Back Hours

"If I meet my kid's needs, I'm starving my creativity. If I feed my creativity, I feel like I'm starving my child."

"When I'm at work, I feel guilty about neglecting my child. If I'm with my child, I feel like I'm missing deadlines and losing earnings to pay for everything she needs."

These are the voices of women struggling to resolve the conflict between their personal and professional lives. For some, striking a balance means cutting back on their work hours in order to accommodate changes in their child's developmental timetable.

"I never was the stay-at-home type," said Carmen, a forty-six-year-old technical illustrator and proud single mother of Terry, her active six-year-old daughter. "When Terry was two, three, even four years old, she was happy to stay at preschool until the place shut down, which was great for me. I knew I couldn't give up my life as an artist and still be happy as a mom." But when Terry got into primary school, Carmen noticed a big change. "She wanted to be a 'pick-up kid.' That's kid lingo for the kid who waits outside for her mom to pick her up right after school every day. She was adamant about not wanting to go to the YMCA, and she didn't want anyone else picking her up. She wasn't at all impressed with my superachieving. She'd watch me dash around and say, 'Slow down, Mom.' She wanted to come home and plant seeds and watch the garden grow. She wanted to bake bread with me.

"I finally cut back to twenty-five hours a week six months ago," Carmen said. "I still have a creative life apart from motherhood, and Terry is a much happier kid. That's what counts. Having a child was my impulse to keep myself grounded and connected to the human race. Now I have to be a human being every day at three o'clock."

Carmen hopes that the time will come when she can resume working full time again. "In a few years, my daughter won't *want* to see me after school," she laughed. "She'll want to be with her girlfriends, or be doing some kind of sports. I

The trouble with the rat race is that even if you win, you're still a rat.

LILY TOMLIN

can live with this scaled-back work schedule knowing it won't last forever." Before Carmen left my office, she wondered, "How do other women work this one out?"

Carmen's question became the heated topic of the next Wednesday night support group. What became apparent as the women present shared their stories was that they were having to make individual judgment calls concerning parenting and careers without the benefit of any formula to follow.

Mara described herself as "blowing in the wind" during her twenties and early thirties. By thirty-five, she had focused on becoming a psychotherapist, and by the time she married in her early forties, her career was well established. "I was a late bloomer. Right after I got married, I had two children, two years apart. I arrived at a high point in my career at the same time my daughters arrived. I hired a nanny after the birth of my first daughter and went right back to work. It never occurred to me to do otherwise. But one day after my second daughter was born, I broke down and wept because I couldn't remember my first daughter as a baby. At that point, I had to choose between working even harder and making a name for myself in my field, or spending more time with my kids. My two-year-old always wanted to stay home and sobbed her little heart out every time I dropped her off at the babysitter. By the time I saw my first client, I had already been through my *own* major crisis."

Mara leaned back and relaxed into her chair as she continued. "My husband and I talked it over, and since he earns more than I do anyhow, we decided that I'd cut back to fifteen

> Motherhood highlights the aberrant ways we live as a culture. No other culture expects one woman to suddenly be endowed with all this knowledge on how to raise a child. No other culture expects her to do it alone.
>
> LAURA, FORTY-FOUR-YEAR-OLD MOTHER OF TWO-YEAR-OLD LIAM

hours a week. It's wonderful to see what a huge difference our decision has made to my older daughter. I still think about the creative potential I'm not getting to fulfill, and there are strings of days when I feel like I'm in a perpetual cut-your-losses mode, but so far they have been balanced by the deep pleasures of having children and watching them grow. I guess I just wasn't willing to miss out on the years when my kids are so young and so precious."

Olympia was quiet for a moment and then sat forward in her chair. "Look," she said earnestly, "I never wanted to be a full-time parent. I'm not cut out for it. So even if I were coparenting, which I'm not, I'd still want to work outside the home." Olympia made the decision to have a child alone using anonymous donor sperm and gave birth to her daughter when she was forty-four. She took the first three months off and then resumed work full time for the next three years as a computer programmer "because I really needed the paycheck and the benefits. But I was getting just too frazzled, doing a poor job of keeping up with the day-to-day chores, never getting bigger projects done, and not relaxing on the weekends with my kid."

Two months ago Olympia cut back to a four-day workweek. "My daughter is now in school five days a week," she continued. "The extra day at home alone allows me to get more personal things done. It gives me quiet time to myself and lets me think through priorities so I can focus on what's important. Since I have time at home with and without my daughter, I can appreciate her more on the weekends and evenings. I'm earning less money, which means I can't buy her as much 'stuff,' but the trade-off is that I'm more relaxed."

Normalizing Our Choices

Your child's needs will change as she grows. If you've decided to scale back on work hours in order to meet these needs, staying flexible about when, where, and how to apply your care and attention will contribute to everyone's well-being. If your toddler is a slow starter in the morning, try to arrange your schedule so you can spend a leisurely hour with her (preferably in your nightgown or pajamas). Then when your pace quickens and your attention divides later in the day, she'll feel cared for and you'll feel less conflicted. If your elementary school-aged child now wants you to pick her up after school and help with homework, if it's possible, consider putting early morning or evening hours into work. The more flexible you can be about when you get the time you need, the more likely it is you'll get it—guilt free—because your family will already have at least some of their needs met first.

> To be really great in little things, to be truly noble and heroic in the insipid details of everyday life, is a virtue so rare as to be worthy of canonization.
>
> HARRIET BEECHER STOWE

Another successful strategy for creatively meeting everyone's needs is to normalize your choices within your own immediate family. For a long time, I was intimidated by the dictum that declared dinnertime to be the ultimate sacred bonding time for families, and woe to the parent who dared violate it. But I've never enjoyed dinnertime. It was the gut-wrenching battlefield of my childhood. So years later, after struggling with guilt and a false sense of obligation to my family, I finally decided that living authentically was a more valuable role model for my daughter than forcing myself to cook and eat a meal I couldn't digest. The good news is that we all love having breakfast together. We make mouth-watering green chile breakfast burritos (a New Mexican specialty), and when we leave for work and for school it is with a great sense of shared time, love, and nourishment. I often use the dinner hour to catch up on work while my husband and daughter enjoy a special dinner for two. These rituals have become what's "normal" within our family: small islands of intimacy and leisure we can count on and cherish within the modern-day sea of deadlines and schedules.

The Somebody I Used to Be

Fueling all the confusion over where we *really* belong—out in the world fulfilling our potential as an individual or at home nurturing the next generation—is the fallout from the Women's Movement. Midlife mamas were raised to believe they could and should Amount to Something. That might have meant becoming a doctor or a lawyer; "mother" wasn't even on the list. From that point of view, staying at home with our children becomes a betrayal of our professional training, in fact, of the Women's Movement itself. Women who contemplate staying at home at the expense of a blossoming career often confess to feeling like a smart woman making a stupid choice. Adjusting to her loss of financial independence as well as society's subtle judgment that she is "wasting her talents" becomes an enormous challenge for the midlife career woman who just might want to be a full-time mom.

Dara came to support group with her beautiful eight-month-old daughter and nursed her to sleep while she spoke. She had moved up the corporate ladder in pharmaceutical sales quickly at a young age. By the time she was thirty-four, she was working fifty to sixty hours a week and traveling 50 percent of the time. "I was very focused on the job thing," she said. "I didn't even have a date for a couple of years. But then a lot of my friends started having babies, and it made me real nervous. My mom had a long history of mental illness, and I was afraid I'd be like her. So I guess I suppressed a lot of my feminine traits."

When Dara was promoted to regional manager, she discovered that she loved nurturing people. "One of the women who reported to me said, 'You know, Dara, you'd be a really good mom.' I started crying because I got in touch with all the feelings I'd suppressed for a long time. Right after that I started dating someone, and we got married a year later. We took this 'Do You Want to Have a Baby?' workshop. My husband was kind of going back and forth and didn't know if he wanted to have kids, but it was starting to feel like something I wanted to do. I was managing a lot of moms who were working part time because of their kids, and I knew I could do that.

"I was making three times as much money as my husband, so once we made the decision to have a family, I thought I'd try working part time from home after the baby was born," Dara said. Her friends had told her she'd have no trouble putting in part-time hours because "all babies do is eat and sleep," and she'd have plenty of time on her hands. "So I started receiving phone calls from work when she was two weeks old," Dara said. "At the same time I ended up in the emergency room because there was some placenta left in me. The baby was crying all the time because she wasn't getting enough to eat, and I was still trying to put in twenty hours a week. I kept thinking I *had* to do the job, and I didn't want to burden the staff. So I'd be nursing and my boss would call and he'd say, 'Well, where are you?' and I'd think, 'I'm not anywhere.' He'd ask me, 'Can you travel?' and I'd say, 'No, I can't travel, I'm nursing.' His attitude was, 'Just

> When I was in high school, my guidance counselor told me that "mother" was not a career choice.
>
> FRIEDA, FORTY-THREE-YEAR-OLD MOTHER OF TWO-YEAR-OLD ELI

drop your kid off and get back to work.' I was so stressed out about not getting my job done that I couldn't relax and enjoy my time with her. I seriously considered hiring someone to be with her full time because I didn't think I was getting the hang of mothering. She had entire days when she cried and I just thought it had to be something wrong with me. I thought I had totally failed and that going back to work was the only thing that would make us both happy. Fortunately," she said smiling down at her contented baby, "I didn't find good childcare."

If I stopped the tapes that said I had to prove something, I'd like to stay at home with my daughter and feed the birds. I could enjoy hanging out. I'm so tied into the image I've created of who I am, I forget that maybe that isn't what I want.

CARLA, FORTY-FOUR-YEAR-OLD MOTHER OF THREE-YEAR-OLD SOPHIE

Dara eventually made the decision to quit her job and be a full-time mother, saying that she realized that she wanted to be home with her child, giving and receiving love in a way no other experience could provide. "But," she notes, "our society doesn't value motherhood, not compared to what I had achieved in my career. I worry about myself—that I didn't realize it sooner. I just assumed I'd just drop her off at four months and go back to work. We're bombarded with that message. You can do it all, you can have it all, a career and a family all at the same time. We don't value people who decide that it's not worth it. We've gotten a little too screwed up with liberation.

"The hard part," she continued, "is when I go to a party and someone says, 'So, what do you do?' I'd say, 'Oh, I've been in business.' Kind of like, 'Here's what I *used* to do.' Like, 'I used to *be* somebody.' It's taken me some therapy and really thinking about this for myself to understand the message from society—that being a nurturer wasn't good enough."

Dara confessed that one major stumbling block in deciding to quit was the issue of giving up her own source of income. "I left home at seventeen and have always made my own money," she said. "Now I'm financially dependent upon my husband. Maybe I could add up everything I do for our family—cooking, cleaning, errands, gardening, paying the bills, childcare, pet care" she said, half laughing and half serious, "and he could cut me a check once a week. That way I won't feel like I have to ask his permission to buy a new bra."

Dara is struggling with one of the consequences of her choice to trade a lucrative career for the role of mother, a full-time job that doesn't even register on the wage scale. Unless this loss of financial independence is openly discussed and acknowledged, it has the potential to be a source of great conflict personally and within family systems. No matter how enlightened a relationship, financial dependence shifts the power dynamics among couples.

Like Dara, many midlife mamas know this is their only shot at mommyhood and they want to hoard it. Often they have arrived at a point professionally where they have nothing left to prove. Although they may have planned to resume work after maternity leave, the immediacy, intimacy, and pleasure of motherhood catches them off guard. Suddenly they find themselves unable to hand over their child for someone else to raise, maybe a woman the baby will learn to love so much she'll end up calling her "mommy." If they have to, they cash in stock options and move to cheaper digs. They trade power lunches for Happy Meals. They play hide and seek, they play Legos *one more time* because they know only too well how quickly the years pass, and that their kids will be grown in the blink of an eye.

But still they speak conspiratorially about what they miss: discretionary income, an office on the twenty-second floor with corner windows, predictable time given over to concentration and creativity, adult conversation, gossip around the water cooler, lunch with the girls, pride in accomplishments, and as one woman put it, "having people actually listen to what I say and do what I ask." And while these women all agree that nothing matters more at this point in their lives than being with their children, they miss being valued and having a purpose in our society that offers very little support or respect—let alone 401(k) benefits or Social Security—to women who curtail their working lives and choose to be "just" a mother.

Midlife moms who stay at home with their children don't regret the decision, but often report the burnout that comes from feeling isolated and lacking in community support. When extended families were the norm, there was always a grandma or auntie to fill the role of second or third mama, but in our one family/one house culture, filling this deficit can be a challenge. Women who have traveled to other countries see innovative new ways of thinking about raising children. In Israel, there are drop-in centers for preschool age children that are free to all families, even when there is a stay-at-home mom. In Norway, working mothers can take almost a year off with pay after giving birth and three years with a guarantee of the same job. The French have universal preschool. A forty-nine-year-old midlife mother who went trekking in Nepal with her husband and eight-year-old daughter marveled that the communal support was so intact she could leave her child at the lodge to play with the village children while she went for an adventure by herself or with a companion. She kept saying to me, "This is how it should be. Now how do I create this at home?"

Creating Support

The important thing to know about yourself is what kind of support you need. If you are an at-home mother and are beginning to feel cut off from outside stimulation and adult contact, put up notices seeking other moms who might be interested in swapping childcare or planning outings with the kids. Check out the local toddler classes as a way to get out of the house and meet other women. If you find that you're meeting younger mothers (a common experience) and have less in common with them than you do with your best girl-friend, that's fine. Keep your eye on the goal—to create mutual support and avoid isolating yourself at home with small children.

Hiring a sitter from the local high school or college for a few hours a week can be just the support you need. Use that precious time to meet a friend, read, go shopping, get your nails done, fill in the blank—whatever you need and want to do.

Liza knew that maintaining her career in publishing was a priority, so after the birth of her twins she and her husband hired a live-in nanny. "I was lucky to be in a position to afford help," she said. "I watched my mother have a nervous break-down trying to raise three of us on her own, and I was afraid I'd lose it too if I didn't have support."

Hiring live-in help is one way women who can afford it create support and achieve a balance between work outside the home and parenting. So is paying for quality toddler care or preschool, often run by the very women who have chosen to stay at home with their children, a real win-win for everyone.

Other creative options include choosing to live with another family with children. Childcare and adult conversa-tions are built-in benefits. Something as simple as calling a friend when you need someone to understand what you're feeling can be enormous support. Something as challenging as organizing a rotating neighborhood drop-in center for cooper-ative childcare can have long-term positive effects on the entire neighborhood.

Often the best support is the kind you can give yourself by knowing what your stress point is, and then working to eliminate it. If having to cook meals when you come home is your breaking point, consider cooking in large batches over the weekend. Or if you're a food purist, try lowering your standards and discover the wonders of take-out. I never realized just how stressful grocery shopping with my daughter was for me until a girlfriend sent me a birthday card. On the outside of the card it read, "Happy Birthday! I wish you one of life's greatest pleasures . . ." and on the inside, "Grocery shopping without your kid!" That did it. When even my friends could identify a high-stress area of my life, I resolved to leave my girl with friends, neighbors, or my partner whenever I could when I went to the store in order to avoid the constant, draining battles over sugared cereals and one more set of press-on nails. It wasn't a huge change on the outside, but it helped to steer me clear of my flash point at least once a week. Do yourself and your family a favor: take a moment and identify your least favorite, stress-filled part of the day or week, and then make a sincere effort to rally the support you need to create new routines and patterns.

> When I get home at night, there's the 6:30 rule. No one can ask me anything or tell me anything or make any demands on me for a half an hour. That time is completely my own to make the transition from work to home life.
>
> DENISE, FORTY-NINE-YEAR-OLD MOTHER OF EIGHT-YEAR-OLD TWINS, AUSTIN AND CATHERINE

Ain't Nobody Happy If Mama Not Happy

It should be obvious by now that this chapter is not going to end with me telling you conclusively that there is One Right Way to Work and Parent, or providing you with a handy twelve-step program to follow. Women's stories are varied, often contradictory, and don't support that kind of black or white thinking. Some mothers would perish without the intellectual and creative stimulation their careers provide, others thrive on spending all their time with the kids they waited years to parent.

Each decade has spawned its own "scientific" studies that proliferate like pox in women's magazines, either shaming or applauding a woman for her role in the workplace. We swing between labeling work "bad" for children and the women who pursue it "selfish," to its dizzying opposite of granting sainthood to the women who sacrifice themselves to stay home with the kids, but beware of stereotypes. Some mothers dutifully stay home and neglect their children, others work and have time and energy left over to enjoy them.

One can only wonder at the economic forces that are served in our society by such radically shifting attitudes toward the role of work and motherhood in a modern woman's life. Reading these studies, I am always left with the nagging sense that I am supposed to realign my values and side with the current definition of the "good" mother and repudiate the "bad." But one of the advantages of parenting at midlife is having witnessed these pendulum swings several times in as many decades. I suggest that the possibility now exists for us as older, wiser mothers to take charge of defining what's important to us as professionals and as mothers, and to seek collective solutions to the dilemma that makes working and parenting so either/or.

Women in the workplace are redefining success to include more flexible hours, job sharing, part-time work, telecommuting, and the option of working from home.

> I always want to stop the cars with the damn bumper stickers that say "It Takes a Village to Raise a Child" and ask them if they'd like to put their money where their mouth is, and baby-sit Saturday night.
>
> GLORIA, FORTY-SEVEN-YEAR-OLD MOTHER OF THREE-YEAR-OLD AMBER

Working Mother magazine, dedicated to the premise that women shouldn't have to sacrifice the goal of being a successful employee or executive for being a mother, publishes an annual list of the one hundred companies most committed to helping moms balance careers with the rest of their lives. For a growing number of women, self-employment offers a viable alternative to the "work or stay at home" dilemma. In increasing numbers, they are making the switch to home-based businesses, often drawing on the skills they sharpened during the years they worked outside the home. They seek greater control over their lives and a humane schedule that accommodates both their need to parent thoughtfully and their calling to work purposefully.

What exactly did getting a job in corporate America have to do with us evolving as women? The whole issue of self-respect and setting healthy boundaries seems more central to the evolution of female consciousness. It's the simple things like learning to preserve our own space, dignity, and self-respect that matter.

SUSAN, FIFTY-TWO-YEAR-OLD MOTHER OF TEN-YEAR-OLD ERIN

I hope the stories shared here have helped resolve some of the conflict you may have about the choices you've made. The truth is, none of the options we have available to us are stress free, and none flourish without some price to pay. The challenge is learning how to honor our choices and live creatively with their contradictions and paradoxes. Once we come to recognize that we are, by default, dealing with political and social structures that have failed to keep pace with our entry into the workforce, we can stop viewing our difficulties as personal inadequacies and help to create the solutions that will spring up in communities and neighborhoods like flowers through the concrete.

The Journey Book

THE CHOICES I'VE MADE

The following questions are Things to Think About. That means when you have the time, pick one of them, and write for fifteen minutes as a way to access some of the feelings you may have concerning the choices you've made.

1. How did you arrive at your current work/parent arrangement? Was it dictated by financial necessity? What other motives may have played a part?

2. What, if any, are the changes you might like to make in this arrangement?

3. Do you judge yourself for wanting to make these changes? For example, "selfish" for wanting to (go back to) work, or "irresponsible" for wanting to work less?

4. Are there unspoken agreements with others in your life that keep you locked into patterns and expectations you might wish to change?

5. What does your family need most from you? How might you arrange your schedule to accommodate this need?

LETTER TO MY CHILD

When you have a quiet moment, write a letter (one you needn't send) to your child and tell him or her why you've made the choices you have concerning work and motherhood. What has been your greatest sacrifice and your greatest reward? If you had the chance to choose over again, what, if anything, would you do differently and why? What's the one thing you hope your child will grow up to understand about the choices you have made?

COLLECTIVE SOLUTIONS

Let your imagination roam free. Have you ever considered other ways of living and raising your family? Have you read about or heard about other cultures that take a more collective approach to child rearing? Write for five minutes, stream of consciousness, about the small steps you might take within your community to implement some of these ideas.

CHAPTER FOUR

Midlife Moms and the Infertility Mill

My Eggs

I sit across from the brooding young man
and examine the brush of his eyebrows
the unruly whiskers that shoot
over the rim of his glasses.
I hate this doctor whom I've paid exorbitantly
to give me bad news.
I twirl my rings, lick my lips, straighten
the seam of my sweater sleeve
as I line him up in the crosshairs of my gaze.
He shuffles my test results absently
across his desktop.
"Your eggs are old," he muses,
tapping his fingers in an A-frame
of protection in front of his paisley tie.
"The good ones are gone.
You're not like the young, who simply
throw their ovulations away.
They never miss a dozen eggs."
He chuckles at his little grocery joke.

I picture myself at 15, frizzed and barefoot
plucking 12 eggs from an egg carton
recklessly tossing them one by one
each month of my cycle into fields
of lush green expanse.
Where each egg lands, a flowering magenta plume
shimmers, surrounded by bluebells.
The earth is fertile, the babies abound.
My young eggs have fallen, spent
in my heedless youth.
"A few good eggs are all you need."
His words hang in the interval between us,
a black cloudbank of news reshaping my landscape.

A large, frail egg sails off my lap
pale dirigible drifting out into the dark universe
between our chairs.
Cracked like raku porcelain, hundreds
of tiny silver lines thread their way
across its pearly expanse, this egg the last
and the best of my collection.
It hangs between the young doctor and me
daring him to say more.

"You could surely consider an egg donor," he squeezes
through tapping fingers. I imagine my womb
a rental unit for the juvenile eggs
of another, and feel the lines of age
deepen on my face.
I watch the insulted dirigible
dart back and forth along the pathway
of my doctor's words and feel rain in the air.
There will not be a baby.

I stand and carefully scoop my prized egg
into my bag, where it roots
around a bit before settling down
on a nest of loose kleenex at the bottom.
I leave the office bent forward,
older, careful not to swing the bag
as I climb the three sets of stairs
to the street.

—CHRISTY SHEPARD

Nothing quite compares to the shock, disbelief, humiliation, and outrage an older woman feels when she discovers that no matter how young she may look or feel, she can't conceive because her eggs are, simply put, too old. She was born with her lifetime quota of eggs—about three hundred thousand of them—already inside her ovaries, but this supply has been systematically reduced by ovulation and has deteriorated because of environmental pollutants, X rays, chemicals, medications, drugs, additives in food and water, and the toxins to which she has been exposed. Because of these factors, a woman who has planned on becoming pregnant later in her reproductive life may find that, past a certain point, she is unable to do so because the viability of her eggs has been compromised.

What follows learning of her infertility may be a period of sadness, anger, frustration, and isolation, combined with a profound sense of grief for what will never be. She may revisit her past and try to determine when, where, and why she made the decision to postpone motherhood. All her past decisions concerning education, career, and personal opportunities come up for reexamination. Guilt and remorse may surface now over an earlier abortion, and her infertility may seem like "punishment," no matter how right the decision may have been at the time. Working through all of these painful feelings may take a month, a year, or a lifetime. Many women close this chapter of their lives by moving forward with plans to adopt a child. Others place their longing for a biological child into the hands of a team of doctors, nurses, and laboratory assistants, and enter the complex medical labyrinth called Assisted Reproductive Technology, or ART to the initiated. With ART, she will submit herself to treatments ranging from low to high tech: temperature charts, nasal sprays, hormone injections, steroids, and surgeries that will most often leave her scarred, weary, and fundamentally altered.

I would have given up the dream of Prince Charming a lot sooner if I knew my fertility was declining.

CAITLIN, FORTY-SEVEN-YEAR-OLD MOTHER OF FOUR-YEAR-OLD JUDD

She submits to these daily invasive procedures because she knows it is her last chance to bear a child. She submits because all of the competency, training, education, and success she has achieved cannot help her attain her goal. She submits because either suddenly, or over many years, her longing for a child has grown and now nothing else seems worth wanting. Perhaps she has had several miscarriages, a string of all the wrong partners, a failed first marriage, or no partner at all. Now as she faces the beginning of perimenopause and the end of her childbearing years, she is looking at the distinct possibility that she will live the second half of her life childless and is willing to move heaven and earth to alter this unacceptable outcome.

Women who have successfully undergone infertility treatments come to First-Time Moms over Forty support groups with a bittersweet mixture of awed gratitude for the child they eventually bore and enduring issues about the toll—physical, emotional, financial, and spiritual—the treatments took on their lives. Some feel betrayed by their biology and angry that while they pursued the dream of "having it all," their fertility was in steady, stealthy decline. If they were used to being in control, they remember how helpless they felt to affect the outcome of their treatments as they submitted to doctors with no sense of urgency or a false sense of optimism. They tell stories of spending a lifetime's savings on a year's worth of treatments and recount their grief when they faced the probability that, at best, one child is all they would bear. They talk of the shock they felt when they learned that because of multiple implants that "took," they were carrying twins or triplets.

Even for these women who bore children after infertility, there is a lingering aftermath. They have lost time and resources that can never be recaptured. They may always feel different from other women for whom conception came easily, and they may fear retribution if they forget to be grateful even for a moment. But while the experience of infertility doesn't go away, while these women may never "get over it," they do learn to "get on with it," to heal and restore those parts of themselves that have been impacted by infertility and to find acceptance and resolution for the life they now live.

> It was a complicated road getting to parenthood. The pain of infertility is almost gone for me personally, but I continue to have great compassion for those who are still struggling to have a child.
>
> CARLA, FORTY-SIX-YEAR-OLD MOTHER OF TWO-YEAR-OLD LUKE

A Race against Time

Many women over forty falsely believe that as long as they are still menstruating, they can easily get pregnant, but, as we've seen, the ability to conceive declines with age. For a woman under thirty-five, approximately four out of every five of her eggs has the potential to create a healthy baby. A woman over forty will experience a 50 percent decline in the quality and quantity of her eggs, and by the time she is forty-five, most of her eggs will be defective.

Barbara came to a First-Time Moms over Forty support group and talked openly about her experience with infertility. "I'm a scientist and I didn't know a thing about my eggs aging," Barbara told the group. Now in her mid-forties, she earned her doctorate in geology when she was thirty-three, and then enjoyed working and traveling for the next several years. She married her husband at thirty-eight, and then tried to have a baby for two years before she went to a fertility specialist. "He explained that not all eggs are good eggs and that mine were simply too old. He recommended using in vitro fertilization [IVF] because he said there was no time to waste." Barbara and her husband did choose to use IVF and after two cycles successfully conceived and delivered a healthy baby boy. "It was a race against time. I would have been devastated if I had been unable to conceive," she said. "How could I have spent all that money on my education and not learned a thing about my declining fertility rate? Everyone needs this information to make an informed decision."

Michelle, who is typical of many women of her generation who grew up believing motherhood was second best, spoke next. "The two things I heard my mother say a million times were, 'Don't grow up to be *just* a mother,' and 'Don't grow up to be *just* a secretary,' which sounded like the worst fate in the world." Michelle decided on a career as a clinical psychologist, and after spending six years in graduate school, she threw herself fully into her work. When she was thirty-five, she joined a dating service and met her husband quickly. "We got married when I was thirty-six, and then we thought we had enough time to wait a couple of years to have kids while we got to know each other. By the time we seriously started trying to have a family, I was thirty-eight. That's when all the infertility problems began, and I started years of treatments. I went through all the standard tests and it turned out I had several things that needed fixing: scarring from an IUD I had when I was younger, a blocked tube, and fibroids. I had two surgeries and then I finally conceived, but it was an ectopic pregnancy. After that I had two miscarriages. There was no single factor that kept me from conceiving—it was the combination that made it difficult."

Michelle paused for a moment before she continued. "As I got older, it got harder and harder," she said. "By the time I was in my early forties, having gone through these surgeries and still not carrying a pregnancy to term, they couldn't find anything else wrong with me. Their final diagnosis was old eggs. The thought that I was never going to have a baby because my eggs were too old was like a death sentence hanging over my head. I even began to wonder why my husband didn't go off with a younger fertile woman."

Michelle and her husband went on to have two children using an egg donor, choosing this option because it meant that their children would be genetically connected to at least one of them. "It never entered my mind that I was sacrificing motherhood for my career," she said later. "I felt like I was doing the right thing, and looking back I don't know what I would have done differently. I was programmed to be the way I was."

My partner and I survived the crisis of infertility together. We cried together, we spent lonely weekends together waiting for test results, we went through invasive procedures together. We are stronger and more committed as a couple than ever before. We have learned to have faith and to trust in miracles.

WINNIE, FORTY-TWO-YEAR-OLD MOTHER OF EIGHT-MONTH-OLD GLORY

Rahina had hung back from participating in the discussion and now chose her words carefully as she began to speak. "Learning that my eggs were too old left me with a long-lasting combination of shame and humiliation," she said. "Even though I had no particular feelings about the doctor up to that point, I suddenly felt very exposed and humiliated in a way I hadn't anticipated. I felt like the way I looked changed in an instant, like I suddenly aged right on the spot. The minute I walked out of his office I felt old and wizened and dry. I started having all these thoughts about the women in the Bible who were barren, women who couldn't bear children. It was really the first time in my white middle-class life that I was confronted with something I might not be able to overcome. I remember getting really angry and thinking, 'Oh yeah? You don't know what you're talking about. I'll take your fertility drugs and I'll show you.'"

Thirty years ago the diagnosis of old eggs would have meant that a woman either chose to adopt children or found other ways to nurture the next generation. Now science offers women—of almost any age—an array of technologies to help overcome infertility and to produce biological children in response to the powerful maternal longing of the human heart.

The Ten-Thousand-Dollar Choice

The new reproductive technologies offer all the blessings and curses of a genie let out of the bottle. On the one hand, they help women who would otherwise be unable to have them bear biological children. On the other hand, they involve varying degrees of invasiveness into a woman's emotional and physical being, and seriously impact her partnership and individual lifestyle.

An older woman entering the world of ART usually undergoes a complete medical evaluation. This may include stimulating her follicles—the fluid-filled sacs that contain the eggs within the ovary—with hormones to determine her "ovarian age" and indicate the probability of a successful pregnancy using any of several fertility options. Treatment recommendations may first include a hysterosalpingogram (HSG) test, which is an X ray of the uterus and fallopian tubes used to diagnose possible tubal blockages and uterine abnormalities. A laparoscopy—a surgical procedure that corrects pelvic adhesions, tubal abnormalities, or endometriosis (a condition in which the cells that normally line the uterus grow on or within the ovaries or fallopian tubes)—may be recommended as well. Once these obstacles to conception are cleared, women may proceed to using fertility drugs like Clomid, Metrodin, and Pergonal, which stimulate egg production, alone or in combination with intrauterine insemination (IUI), an in-office procedure that places sperm directly inside her uterus, or in vitro insemination (IVF). IVF involves inducing ovulation with fertility drugs for the first ten to twelve days of her cycle and then, using the guidance of ultrasound, retrieving these eggs, fertilizing them with the chosen sperm in a sterile dish, incubating them under laboratory conditions for two to three days, and then transferring viable embryos back into the woman with the hope of a successful pregnancy and birth. Since not all embryos successfully implant, multiple embryos are transferred in the hopes of obtaining one live birth, with the consequence that multiple births are always a possibility. This procedure, plus the ten-day wait until pregnancy can be confirmed, is often described as a torturous emotional roller-coaster ride for those involved.

Other techniques include Gamete Intrafallopian Transfer (GIFT), which involves the same procedure as IVF, but implants the egg and sperm in the woman's fallopian tube for natural fertilization; Frozen Embryo Transfer (FET), which involves the transfer of previously fertilized and subsequently frozen embryos; and Egg Donor IVF, which follows the procedure for IVF but uses an egg donated by another (often younger) woman.

But even this astonishing display of technology has its limitations. A woman who chooses IVF has at best about a 20 percent chance of a successful pregnancy in a given cycle. The cost per cycle is about $10,000, and she may need to undergo treatment for several cycles. Insurance coverage is poor or nonexistent.

"When I got to the place of finally knowing that I was infertile, there really wasn't that much choice," one client who successfully conceived with IVF told me. "I was going to spend $10,000 whichever way I looked at it. Ten thousand dollars for IVF, $10,000 for an international adoption, or $10,000 to take an extended trip because I chose to be childless and I couldn't stand to think about it."

Cycles of Hope and Despair

When women share their stories of infertility clinics—invasive procedures that extract and insert, hormone shots with needles big enough for horses, young male interns who haven't got a clue—they swap them with the grim humor of a war story, one survivor to another. "My husband was in the clinic bathroom trying desperately to fill a specimen jar with sperm when a helicopter flew by the window." "When I had run out of money and couldn't afford to do IVF again, the clinic told me I could get frequent flyer miles if I put it on my credit card. That's 10,000 miles!" The timed sex when ovulation is occurring, the mad dashes to clinics over bridges, through tunnels, in sunshine, in snow, these are all part and parcel of the infertile woman's experience. The waiting, the hoping, and the despair are often followed by the decision to try just one more time. These are the stories women tell each other, glad for someone who understands.

"I felt like I had bought a one-way ticket to hell," Diana, a forty-six-year-old writer confided to the group. "My moods shifted between hope and despair within days, sometimes within hours. Not only were the drugs affecting me, but the two weeks after an IVF treatment and before I got the results were brutal. I was on a ragged roller-coaster ride. I went up, allowing myself to feel hopeful, and then I'd come crashing down into despair, dreading the next negative test result. I became reclusive and envied every pregnant woman I saw." Diana went through four IVF cycles before she conceived her son, Nick, who is now two.

Rahina continued telling us her story. She began taking fertility drugs once she learned that her eggs were too old to conceive naturally. A single lesbian woman, she had tried for several years to conceive using artificial insemination with sperm from the local sperm bank before she made this decision. "I never thought I'd need to use drugs. I thought it was just a matter of time before I got pregnant. But once I realized I couldn't, I decided to try Clomid. I had a very bad mood disturbance from it. I kept calling the doctor and saying, 'I have no libido. I'm too paranoid and anxious to go out of the house. I'm depressed and crying all the time.' He'd say, 'Keep trying, you want to have a baby, don't you?'" Rahina took Clomid for several more months. Ultrasound confirmed that she was producing eggs, so she continued testing her urine and inseminating when there was a surge of hormones. When no pregnancy resulted, she chose to progress to Pergonal, an ovulation-inducing hormone that she had to inject twice a day. "I was scared to take Pergonal because it was stronger than Clomid. It didn't affect my moods as badly, but I could tell that it was throwing me out of whack. I didn't have my usual energy and my body ached like I had the flu for half of the month. I felt so driven during that time, giving myself these shots twice a day and then going for an ultrasound to check my follicles in the middle of the month. I was completely caught up in the machinery of the fertility specialists, and I couldn't face the disappointment of not being pregnant if I stopped trying. I couldn't imagine what else I was going to do with my life."

Rahina knew that she had to stop the treatments for her emotional and physical well-being, and she promised herself that she would, after one last try. She conceived her son on her final round of insemination when she was forty-four.

Barbara, the geologist who ultimately conceived with IVF, described having her follicles retrieved at the infertility clinic with "a guy in the next room yelling 'egg' or 'no egg' as he inspected each one of them under a microscope. She returned home and kept in touch with the clinic on a daily basis to follow the progress of her embryos. "I felt like I had, not real babies, but these things of mine living outside my body in a test tube somewhere. My husband and I followed the growth, and it was as if I were pregnant, but not really, which is funny because when I was growing up my mother always said you couldn't be just a little bit pregnant."

Unlike many of the women in my support groups who chose to postpone motherhood, Jenny, who is now forty-two and the proud mother of a nine-month-old daughter, started trying to get pregnant when she was thirty-one. After two years, her doctor recommended IVF but she was appalled; she felt too young and the procedure was too invasive. She spent the next several years changing her diet, going for acupuncture treatments, and coaxing her husband into drinking bitter Chinese herbs. When that didn't work, she tried Clomid for four cycles, then a laparoscopy, then Pergonal, and several inseminations, all of which failed. "Every time I went to the clinic I saw a different doctor," she told us. "They weren't familiar with my case, they never really knew who I was, and I didn't feel like they were able to handle a lot of my emotional issues. It was stressful talking to someone different every time; I didn't really feel like I could connect with any of them. They kept encouraging me to do IVF, which I just couldn't afford." She explained to us that her husband had two grown children from a previous marriage and "was just going along with what I wanted. I was the one who was intent on getting pregnant. Early on if I had gotten pregnant, it would have been fine with him, but once we started having problems he felt like, 'Well, let's just not have a kid.' But that wasn't okay with me."

Jenny made the decision to leave the "infertility rat race" and resume her career as a dancer. She went on tour for a year, but the prospect of starting infertility treatments all over again made her depressed and anxious. She returned home and despite her misgivings, did just what she thought she'd never do: she decided to do IVF. "I called my mother and asked her for the money to do it. She was great about it and gave me the money. Since I wasn't limited by my insurance company, I could see the same doctor every time. It made a huge difference. He asked me specific questions that had more to do with my emotional life than my physical life; he asked me where I was at with all I had gone through. I broke down in his office. I told him that I felt like nobody really understood the level of my frustration and disappointment because they never took the time. I told him that we had spent thousands of dollars and needed someone to understand that I didn't have another $10,000 sitting in the bank. Having the treatments not work was devastating. It wasn't as simple as just trying again." Jenny's voice filled with emotion and she sat silently for a moment. "I felt like he really heard that," she continued, "so I did IVF. It was horrible, invasive, and painful, and it didn't work. I said I'd never do it again, but I did, and when I went in for the results the second time I was prepared to let everything go. I had a good marriage and wonderful work, and I just wanted my body back. That's when I found out I was pregnant.

"I'm pretty easy going generally speaking," she said thoughtfully. "But because it had taken me so long to get pregnant, and because it had cost me so much physically, emotionally, and financially, once I got pregnant it was really hard for me just to enjoy the pregnancy. I spent the first three months convinced I was going to miscarry. Every time some little thing happened, I was a basket case. Then when I delivered, there were all these complications—it didn't go smoothly at all. The baby was in intensive care and I couldn't hold her for twenty-four hours. There was not one thing about getting pregnant, being pregnant, or the actual delivery itself that felt 'normal'—it was all totally stressful. Now I look at my baby and say it was worth it. I'm so glad I did everything I could to have a baby because I didn't want to turn around at forty-five and regret not trying harder to have a child."

Two Strollers, Two Cribs

Fertility drugs, which cause multiple follicles to develop, are needed to successfully retrieve multiple eggs during an IVF treatment. They are also one of the causes of multiple births, even when the drugs are used apart from IVF treatment. A fertility doctor using IVF to treat an older woman's infertility will seek to optimize success rates for pregnancy by transferring a large number of embryos, usually more than six, in the hopes of offsetting any problems that might exist in the quality of her eggs. It is increasingly common for a woman to go from the anguish of infertility to the bounty of having more children than she might have planned for or ever dreamed possible.

A 1999 study from the Centers for Disease Control and Prevention documented the unprecedented increase in the twin/multiple birth rate among American women over the age of forty. During the last seventeen years, the twin rate rose 63 percent for women aged forty to forty-four, but the greatest increase in twin rate was among women aged forty-five to forty-nine, with an astonishing rate increase of nearly 1,000 percent from 1980 (when this age group bore only eight sets of twins) to 1999. In fact, mothers aged forty-five to forty-nine bore more twins in 1997 alone than during the entire decade of the 1980s. But lest you think the trend stops here, in 1997 there were fifty twin births and thirteen triplet births for mothers aged fifty to fifty-four. It is worth noting that in England and France, the law restricts to three or less the number of embryos that a woman may have put in her uterus.

I couldn't believe that I, Ms. Infertility, had become the mother of twins. I hadn't even been able to manage one pregnancy. The thought of more than one seemed preposterous!

EVELYN, FORTY-SEVEN-YEAR-OLD MOTHER OF TWO-YEAR-OLD TWINS, AMANDA AND APRIL

"I knew there was a risk that I could have more than one," Karen said, "but it's all just an idea until the reality hits." After three unsuccessful rounds of fertility drugs and inseminations, Karen, a forty-three-year-old environmental lawyer and her fifty-year-old husband, Jay, turned to IVF and conceived during their first cycle. When they went for their ultrasound, Karen remembers that the doctor and nurses were "quite silent. I broke the silence and said, 'It's twins, isn't it?' The doctor nodded and tried to make a joke and said, 'Well, you wanted children, didn't you?'" Karen and her husband sat stunned for a moment. "Then we went out into the waiting room where we had waited all those other times," she said. "Jay's eyes were big and unfocused, like he was trying to register what had just happened. We went home and were in complete shock for about a week. We kept saying, 'What have we done?' We imagined two of everything. Two strollers, two high chairs, two cribs. The turning point was when I woke up about a week after that and had some bleeding. I called the doctor and he said, 'You better come to the hospital right away.' Suddenly we went from, 'Oh my God we're having two', to 'Oh my God, we're not going to lose one, are we?' It had been such a hard road to get to that point and then the reality that we might lose one was awful." Karen and Jay spent six nerve-wracking hours waiting for their ultrasound, which eventually confirmed the beating of two healthy hearts. "From that moment on, our emotional commitment was really strong; we knew we wanted both of them."

I cried when I found out I was having twins, knowing a fair amount about how much work taking care of children can be. Plus, I was living in a fifth floor walk-up, a tiny apartment. When I was six months pregnant I decided to move to a house with a backyard. Now I feel so lucky that I have twins despite how much work it is at times. Having two makes it easier to be satisfied with my family size as it is.

MEGAN, FORTY-FIVE-YEAR-OLD MOTHER OF TWO-YEAR-OLD TWINS, KEVIN AND GRACE

Karen recalled discussing the probability of having multiples with her doctor when she had five embryos transferred. "I remember saying, 'Isn't that a bit extreme?' But he said he had to consider my age and the viability of my eggs relative to the number of embryos he put back. I know these clinics depend upon their success rate," she said. "Their marketability is based on the results they produce, so I knew there was even a risk of triplets. But we had been through so many cycles of dashed hopes that we considered the twins the greatest miracle of our lives. I was glad to play the hand that had been dealt me."

While multiple births may seem at first glance to make economic sense for an older woman, a kind of two-for-the-price-of-one, given the expense of fertility treatments and her race against time, any multiple gestation is a high-risk pregnancy. There is an increased threat of premature delivery, and most women carrying multiples are confined to strict bed rest during the second half of their pregnancies. Those who aren't ordered to bed remain virtually inert, trying to carry their babies as close to term as possible. Multiple births may also mean the spontaneous loss of one or more of the fetuses, with one or several of the others surviving. But perhaps even more difficult is having to make the decision to reduce a high-risk multiple pregnancy to a singleton or twins because of the risk it poses to the health of the mother or because one or more of the fetuses has been determined to be genetically abnormal, or for both of these reasons. This process, called selective reduction, is usually done before the end of the first trimester and involves, under the guidance of ultrasound, injecting a salt

Watching the triplets roll around on the floor together, watching them develop their own special language together has been wonderfully sweet and fun for me and my husband. We think that having only one baby would be very uneventful and boring!

JILL, FORTY-TWO-YEAR-OLD MOTHER OF ELEVEN-MONTH-OLD TRIPLETS, SEAN, JACK, AND ERIC solution directly into one or more of the fetuses, which is then gradually reabsorbed into the mother's body.

Having to choose selective reduction can feel like a moral minefield, especially to a woman who has tried so desperately to get pregnant. During her second IVF cycle, Barbara's doctor recommended transferring six of the embryos back into her, but her fears of a multiple birth led her to choose four instead. All four embryos attached. After two months, one of the fetuses spontaneously aborted leaving triplets, two of whom had genetic abnormalities. "We had to decide whether or not to undergo selective reduction," she said. "We stayed up for twenty-four hours phoning about a hundred of our friends and family. We finally decided to do it because my husband's mom said, 'You have one normal child, give him a chance.' There was still the possibility that I'd miscarry the last baby," she said, "so I really didn't allow myself to have very high expectations."

> We are the hero of our own story.
>
> MARY MCCARTHY

Barbara delivered her healthy baby boy by C-section at thirty-five weeks. "I was so elated and grateful," she said. "But the excruciating part was having to make a life and death decision about the other two babies. It felt like the right thing to do, but my husband and I had to face that decision on our own. It was the hardest choice I ever had to make."

Grieving Our Losses, Healing Our Hearts

And so they lived happily ever after. Or did they? Women who struggled with infertility and beat the odds to become first-time mothers over forty count themselves among the fortunate; most know women who weren't so lucky. They constantly refer to the miracle that brought their children into existence and to the blessing of having a family with whom to share the fullness of their heart. But given all of this bounty, how do they explain lingering feelings of loss and sadness?

The losses are real and they are many. There is the obvious loss of time, resources, and goals put on hold while treatment was pursued. But there are other immeasurable losses, like the second or third pregnancy that most likely will never occur, babies lost in utero or in miscarriage, the loss of the continuity of our genetic line if an egg donor was used, and the loss of our innocence as we face our vulnerability and the knowledge that not all things are within our control.

For some, the consequence of having lived through the infertility experience is a limited ability to express frustration and disappointment. It's as if she made an imaginary bargain: "If I'm allowed to have this child, I *promise* I'll never yell. I'll always be available. I'll always be giving, gracious, generous, and loving." But what comes along with this promise is the unspoken fear: "If I ever let up on my part of the bargain and admit I'm tired or angry, I'll be punished with the loss of my cherished child."

For all of these women, celebrating life and grieving lost possibilities are the poignant lasting legacies of infertility.

When June bolted from her small Southern town as a young adult, she broke the family pattern of marrying young and having at least a half dozen children. By her late thirties, she had put herself through medical school and established a pediatric practice in a small rural town in New Mexico. When she and her husband tried unsuccessfully for several years to conceive a child, she chose to do IVF and spent two years and all their savings in treatment. June had a healthy baby boy when she was forty-four, and now at forty-seven says, "I feel like I'm just getting started having babies, like I should be thirty-two. How did I suddenly get to the end of the road? My husband has grown kids and doesn't want any more. Last night we stood in the nursery and I wept. I told him, 'Hey, I never got to be young and nest with you. I'm not ready to be old yet. Let's put up the crib and have another baby.'"

At forty-seven, June is struggling to come to terms with the choices she's made in her life. As a thirty-year-old medical student, she conceived a child she felt she couldn't adequately care for. After weeks of agonizing, she made the difficult decision to have an abortion. Now, as she realizes that she is at the end of her fertile years, she says, "I really believed I had to deny one part of myself to get what I thought was important in life. But now when I see young women in my clinic who are considering abortion, I don't try to talk them out of it, but I do tell them about my years of infertility. How could I have been so closed to the beauty and mystery of life? Who decided that the worst thing that could happen to a young woman is to have kids?"

Michelle, who believed motherhood was second best to her career as a clinical psychologist, conceived her two children with the help of an egg donor. "Most of the time I don't think about it at all," she said. "I love them with all my heart. But sometimes I notice how much they look like my husband and not at all like me, and it's a painful reminder that they're not my genetic children. I wonder about the woman whose egg my husband fertilized. Did she have any more children? Do my children have half-siblings they don't even know about?"

Karen, the environmental lawyer and Jay, her husband, became parents of twins after one IVF cycle. Six unused but viable embryos were subsequently frozen. Now at forty-five, Karen feels she is realistically too old to have any more children, especially given the distinct possibility of another multiple birth through IVF, but the issue continues to come up since the birth of the twins: maintaining the embryos in their frozen state requires the annual consent of her and her husband.

"So we get this letter every year, and it's like 'Greetings! Do you want to renew your embryo-freezing contract for another year?' And there are all these boxes to check. If one of us dies, who gets the embryos? Do they get thawed and destroyed? Do we want to donate them to a childless couple? On and on. It feels like we're making life and death decisions over our corn flakes and coffee," Karen said. "If I don't renew and I let my embryos die, it's like admitting that I'll never have another child. So far, we just renew for another year and keep our options open."

Karen knows that growing older is a fact of life, but she is tempted by the new reproductive technologies that seductively promise to extend her fertility time line by at least a decade. This temptation seems particularly endemic in our society that elevates youth to the pinnacle of desirability, shuns its elders as no more than nuisances, and views aging primarily as a disease that can be cured rather than an inevitable part of the life cycle.

Anna suffered four miscarriages before she gave birth to her son. Too old to try again, she and her husband are doting parents to their only child. "But it's odd," Anna said. "Sometimes I say I have to get home to the kids. I think I'm talking about all those babies I lost. I gave them names. I imagined what they'd look like. It's as if my heart and my home still feel a little bit empty without them."

> It's true that my years of infertility took their toll on me, but they also left me with a deep sense of joy and wonder. I'll never take my daughter for granted after all the years I struggled to get pregnant. In a way, infertility prepared me for the adventure of parenthood.
>
> FELICIA, FORTY-NINE-YEAR-OLD MOTHER OF FIVE-YEAR-OLD MICAELA

Lingering feelings of sadness and loss are a reality for women who have successfully conceived after infertility. Often, however, they are reluctant to admit to them for fear of sounding ungrateful, though surely these women do not lack for gratitude. Adding to this reluctance is the expectation that "all that is behind you now," which makes admitting to any difficulties all that much harder. But allowing grief into our hearts is like the old Zen proverb: "The way to control a bull is to give it a big pasture." Allowing ourselves to feel our losses without minimizing or judging them is how we heal the wounds we may still be carrying from our years of infertility. Ironically, experiencing grief loosens its grip on us. Feeling our hearts break and then sitting still long enough for grace to find its way in through the cracks is the surest way I know to restore the energy and joy we need to get on with our lives.

> I've gone back to doing yoga every day. I always thought it had to be for an hour. Now that I've scaled down my expectations of what's possible, I do it for ten minutes, and it's become a wonderful part of my daily life.
>
> REBECCA, FORTY-SIX-YEAR-OLD MOTHER OF FIVE-YEAR-OLD ADAM

If you are partnered, you already know that the infertility experience can take its toll on relationships. After years of scheduled sex, emotional highs and lows, and working so hard for what comes naturally to others, you may have forgotten how to connect with each other as a couple. Can you remember the last time you enjoyed a conversation about something other than your child or children, or the last time you held hands and looked at the moon? Now may be the time to recultivate the pleasure you took in each other before you started trying to have children. If you can afford a sitter or can enlist the help of a friend or relative, slip out for a night away and renew your emotional and sexual relationship in peace and quiet.

If you've been blessed with multiples, look for a local support group for parents of multiples, or if one doesn't exist, put up notices and start your own. Check the Internet for information and resources for families with twins or more (see Resources, pages 196–97). Take advantage of these networking opportunities to meet others who share in the wonder and challenges of the world you have entered.

Above all I encourage you, single or partnered, to add, one at a time, those things back into your life that nurtured you before you entered the world of infertility treatments. It need not be something that takes a lot of time or money. Are you still in touch with the friends you knew back then? Do you go out dancing any more? Have you tucked away your frilly clothes in favor of more practical things? Have you continued with your favorite sport or musical instrument? My life B.C.—Before Children—always included rock and roll music and an eclectic collection of outspoken female singers. In particular, I adored Joan Armatrading. Her music accompanied me on all of my road trips solo or with friends. So now my road-trip days are severely curtailed, but I still blast her unmistakable deep, soulful voice when I do the dishes at night. It's loud. The cats slink away and my husband rolls his eyes, but it's a part of my previous life that never fails to restore my spirits. If you're having a hard time remembering what you enjoyed before you became a mother, ask an old friend who knew you back then and see if you can manage to squeeze just a little bit of these pleasures and activities, big and small, into your daily or weekly routines.

Some say that women who use ART to conceive are tampering with nature and that if they had been intended

> One of the ways I nurture myself is by shopping. I'd sooner talk about my marriage problems than tell you how much I spend.
>
> ANITA, FORTY-SIX-YEAR-OLD MOTHER OF THREE-YEAR-OLD JENNA

to be parents, they would have been. But I have seen time and time again that the women who have the courage to go to these extreme measures are moved by, driven by a longing for motherhood that is powerful, cellular, and in fact hardwired into the survival of the species. From that vantage point, all our judgments seem futile and miss the mark by a mile.

The Journey Book

GRIEVING OUR LOSSES, HEALING OUR HEARTS

For this exercise, you'll need three pictures. The first is an actual photograph of yourself that represents the life you led before you tried to conceive, maybe yourself when you were a young career woman, musician, traveler, student. This is the image of "Who I Was."

The second picture represents the pregnancy, childbirth, or motherhood experience you hoped for but did not achieve. It might be a pregnant woman about the age you were when you first tried to conceive, or a mother with several children, or maybe it's a picture of a child who is the same age as the baby you miscarried would be. This picture is called "What I Lost."

The third picture is a photograph that represents you as you are now. It is called "Who I Am Today."

Allow about fifteen minutes for each part of this three-part exercise. It is ideal to do all of them at the same time, but if that's not possible, doing one part at a time is okay.

Glue the first photograph of yourself into your Journey Book, and sit quietly and look at her. Allow the memories of that time in your life to surface. Where were you living, who were your friends, what clothes did you wear, what was your favorite music, who were you dating? Did you think about having children? Remember one especially memorable scene from that time and journey back until you are standing with her in that moment.

Begin writing. Tell her who you are today. Tell her where you live now and who you live with. Talk about the experiences you've had since that time in your life. Tell her about your child (or children) and the joys and sorrows involved in becoming a mother. Tell her about your infertility, knowing all too well that her life path has already been irrevocably chosen. Let her innocence melt your heart, and if tears well up, imagine your wounds being washed with them. In closing, let her know that you honor her choices; they have made you the woman you are today.

Next paste into your Journey Book the picture that represents what you expected from life and what you lost. Begin writing about your losses. Maybe you thought you'd be a young mother, bearing several children in your youth. For some women the loss was of time, money, and energy. Careers were put on hold, and all the resources that might have been directed toward a new home, travel, business goals, or school were channeled into fertility treatments. This isn't the time to worry about not sounding grateful; it's a private moment for you to express your disappointment, anger, or sadness. It's okay to feel cheated, betrayed, outraged. You're feeling it in order to heal it.

Finally paste the photograph or image that represents your life now in your Journey Book. Write about how your losses have shaped you. Describe the strengths you've developed as a result of these losses. These may be a reordered sense of priorities, resiliency, the ability to deal with disappointments and make difficult decisions, new coping skills, a greater sense of compassion for others, a stronger relationship with your partner and friends, and an ability to find joy in the small moments of life. Write about the things you give thanks for every day, and what you most trust and admire about yourself now.

PROMISES AND BARGAINS

Did you make any deals with the universe when you were trying to conceive? Did they involve *always* and *never?* Write yourself a formal release from this agreement and affirm that you are doing your best, that your best is good enough, and that you and your family are surrounded by beneficial forces working toward the highest good of all concerned.

CHAPTER FIVE

The Long Road Home:
Adoption

Could I raise someone else's child? Would I have enough love? On a really deep level there had to be a change in my mind and my emotions to get to the point where I could see that adoption was not just a second choice. Is it different when children look like you? Do you have more tolerance and patience when they are your biological children? Then a friend said, 'Children don't belong to anybody. They belong to the universe. They come from God no matter who they come through.' After that it was easier.

LILLY, FIFTY-YEAR-OLD MOTHER OF EIGHT-YEAR-OLD PAOLA

Women who become first-time mothers in midlife through adoption—single women, women with partners, lesbian or heterosexual women—have usually made their way through a complex emotional and logistical process. Adoption takes time, money, emotional fortitude, and amazing tenacity. Some women make the decision to adopt once their childbearing years are over, some adopt because their fertility was compromised by medical interventions or illness, others choose adoption as a particularly satisfying solution to parenting without adding to the planet's population. If the decision to adopt comes at the end of years of unsuccessful infertility treatments, it almost always involves grieving the biological child who will never be.

Many older women choose foreign adoption over domestic because it is usually easier for women over forty, especially women who are single or lesbian, to successfully adopt through an international agency. Often the adoption takes place through countries that no longer stipulate that their children be placed with heterosexual couples because war, poverty, or limitation on family size has dramatically increased the number of children needing homes. Even so, foreign adoption presents an endless number of bureaucratic hoops to jump through, including fingerprinting for an FBI check, producing birth certificates, divorce decrees, tax returns, financial statements, intimate autobiographical essays, letters of recommendation, and immigration forms for the baby. And sometimes while the wheels of government turn excruciatingly slowly, while days grow into months, babies grow into toddlers. Older children often arrive after having been abused or neglected in orphanages, or from foster families where over time they have bonded and grown attached. They are often labeled "special needs children," and special skills are required to support and nurture them.

Despite all of these hardships, many adoption stories contain a big dose of magic—mothers who "find" their children over great distances and many miles. These mothers talk of this journey in the same language other women describe labor: it was long, it was hard, it was worth it. Sometimes women apply for adoption and then wait a year or two in limbo. But when the phone rings and she learns that her child is due to arrive, motherhood seems to have happened, ironically, in an instant. "I" becomes "we," individuals become families, and women who longed for a child are at long last mothers.

Giving Up and Letting Go

At fifty, Sheila has established herself as a successful psychotherapist in San Francisco. Raised as a Christian Scientist, she said, "I really believed there was nothing I couldn't achieve. I started trying to get pregnant when I was thirty-eight," she said. "When my relationship ended, I decided to go it alone, and I began taking fertility drugs and inseminating. I got pregnant briefly but lost the baby in a car accident. I thought, 'Well, if I did it once, I can do it again,' but I couldn't. I took fertility drugs for seven years but I never conceived again.

"Having a baby became an obsession," Sheila continued. "I felt like I couldn't live if I didn't have a child. I was in therapy at the time and my therapist kept saying that if it was an issue of wanting a child, I could adopt. I remember thinking, 'What do you know?' Adoption for me was really the last straw. My friend said, 'Why don't you date someone who has a little child and then you could parent?' but I knew that wasn't what I wanted to do. During those years I was so reactive, so sensitive to the pregnant women around me and to my friends who were conceiving so easily. Really, I couldn't stand myself. I felt so indulgent. At the end of all this I thought, 'You know, you really have to stop.' For the first time I seriously began considering adopting a child who needed a home. So in that spirit I invited seven of my friends over and asked them to support me in letting go of my addiction to getting pregnant. Two days later I got a call from an old friend who had just adopted a child from Russia, and in that moment

> Adoption gave me the faith in the goodness of the world, the belief that I would be led to what was right for me. I am so grateful for the struggle of infertility because I wouldn't have elected this path myself. I don't have the guts or courage, but by being forced into it I became a better person. I try to remember when things get crazy that everything I need and want is right here.
>
> LYNN, FIFTY-TWO-YEAR-OLD MOTHER OF ELEVEN-YEAR-OLD CASSIDY

I was galvanized. I knew that was what I was going to do. The next week I signed up with an agency and wholeheartedly turned my energies toward adoption.

"I felt so much grief and anguish before I made the decision to adopt," Sheila said. "My family always taught me that you can overcome any obstacle, you just toughen up and push through it. But I had to face the reality that no matter what I did, I wasn't going to have the biological child I had hoped for. I just had to give up and let go. I was in shock, but in a way it was a huge relief once I put all of that behind me. One thing's for sure," she said, "I ended that period of my life on the other side of the invincibility barrier, and no amount of 'mind over matter' could change that."

Life is so constructed, that the event does not, cannot, will not, match the expectation.

CHARLOTTE BRONTË

Sheila arrived at her decision to adopt by facing the developmental task common to people in their forties: "What can I do and what can't I do, what do I give up, and what's realistic?" There is no way to accomplish this task any quicker than the time it takes to get ready. Over time resistance falls away and cherished hopes are grieved and laid to rest. The heart breaks and mends, and then is ready to turn in a new direction.

The Uprooted Child

Once a woman has made the decision to investigate adoption, she may consider adopting an older child, especially if she is single and over forty. She may choose this route if the idea of adjusting to the nonstop needs of a newborn seems too disruptive or demanding, or because she feels particularly well equipped psychologically to raise an older child with whom she can presumably employ the forces of reason. Or she may choose an older child because they are more available for adoption and she doesn't want to wait for motherhood any longer.

Along with her high hopes is the reality that many of these children may have spent years institutionalized and will inevitably suffer shock leaving their familiar surroundings. They may have slept twenty or thirty to a room and now have intense bouts of anxiety if they are expected to sleep alone in their new home. Some children will cling all their waking hours to their new parents fearing yet another loss, while others will maintain their polite reserve for months until they feel secure enough to throw tantrums. Some will experience the developmental delays associated with original language loss, while others will grieve over the loss of cultural identity.

If new parents expect to find only joy and long-awaited fulfillment once they've adopted their child, if they feel they are finally at the end of a long journey, they may find themselves drained and discouraged once they realize that they are actually at the beginning of a very long adjustment process.

She Was Instantly Attached

"I wanted to adopt a child no more than two years old," Sheila said, "but the social worker said I couldn't apply for a child that young because of my age and because I was single. I found out later she had misled me, but at the time I was clinging for dear life to *whatever* she said. I took a month off from work to fill out stacks of paperwork. As soon as I was done, Russia declared a moratorium on adoption that dragged on for fifteen months. After that there was another delay because chicken pox broke out in the orphanage and it was quarantined for two months. I had already been matched up with my daughter, Alexa, and the agency had given me her picture. It was driving me crazy to think about her getting older and older by the day while I sat helplessly at home.

"I left for Russia more than a year and a half after I made the decision to adopt," Sheila said. "I was with a group of four other families, and we all traveled to the orphanage in Siberia together to adopt four little girls who were all friends. These families are still a big part of our lives, and their pictures are in a special place on our refrigerator.

"Alexa's life at the orphanage was stark," Sheila went on. "She had been brought there when she was eight or nine months old, and was four by the time I got her. There were forty kids living at the orphanage with eight caretakers. It was a big drafty building, and even in May the outside temperature was only twenty-eight degrees. The children ate mostly potatoes, cabbage, and beets, and slept twenty to a room. Before we left, there was this ritual where the kids take off all their clothes and leave them at the orphanage, and you dress them with clothes you've brought. They take absolutely nothing with them. Some of the kids had clearly bonded with their caretakers. It was heartbreaking to see them cry as they were saying good-bye, but Alexa really didn't seem to have someone special she was leaving. She just clung to me and was instantly attached."

Alexa continued to cling to Sheila for the next two years. She was terrified of sleeping alone, and followed Sheila everywhere, even into the shower with her clothes and shoes still on. Sheila had used her months of waiting to study Russian, and now could communicate the basics with her daughter. "I could ask her if she wanted some milk, or if she had to pee, and I quickly learned how to say, 'Don't eat any more sugar!'" Sheila struggled alone to adapt to her new role of mother while she coped with never having a moment of solitude. "I didn't realize how spent I would feel by the time I actually arrived at parenting. I was trying to maintain 'life as it used to be' in the face of this huge transition, and it just wasn't working. Alexa was desperate not to be left alone, and I was growing desperate for some time by myself. She was always with me, and I was exhausted from the effort. I finally broke down and asked my friends for help. Once I was more realistic about the support I needed, I could cope with Alexa's needs more realistically too.

"I started trying to get pregnant when I was thirty-eight, and I went to Russia to get my daughter at forty-seven," Sheila mused. "I had to go through all those years of trying to figure out how to get to parenting. It was a very long road home, but I knew that if I didn't have a child I would forever feel a bottomless pit of hunger. When I picked her up, some huge peaceful feeling replaced the anguish of all those years. No matter how hard it's been, I know I did the right thing because I don't have that longing anymore."

If you've adopted an older child who has lived under traumatic conditions, you already know that it requires an enormous amount of stamina and understanding on your part. Creating a support network for yourself is essential, and it usually means overcoming decades of independence and learning to ask for help. Unless you are willing to occasionally acknowledge your need for support, the only thing you will manage to keep intact will be your pride. Trust me on this one, everything else will suffer.

Asking for help might mean enlisting your friends and family to take your child for a few hours, a day, or even an overnight. It might mean swapping childcare and baby-sitting with a friend. It might mean creating more flexibility at work so that you have an hour to yourself before you go home. It might even mean rearranging your living situation. One married client with a six-year-old adopted daughter from South America rented part of her house to a single mother with a teenage son in exchange for childcare and housekeeping. "It was that, or go out in a blaze of exhaustion," she said.

The Parent Network for Post-Institutionalized Children (see Resources, page 192) offers support programs and newsletters that may help you link up with who and what you need for physical and emotional support.

> The support system I've developed with friends, other mothers, and other adoptive families serves as a pressure release for me. It's a resource for talking things over, a place where I can be honest. I'm someone who needs to be able to talk and bitch and moan!
>
> GINA, FIFTY-YEAR-OLD MOTHER OF FIVE-YEAR-OLD NICOLAS AND THREE-YEAR-OLD MIA

If you know you need support but don't know exactly what to ask for, or are so used to doing everything for yourself that the notion of someone giving you a helping hand is foreign, take an index card and write the word HELP on it in big bold letters. Tape it somewhere you'll see it every day, and when you do, say HELP out loud. Imagine that you're talking to your Fairy Godmother. Confess to her that you could really use a hand, and would she please deliver? This works even if you don't yet know how to name the kind of support you are in need of. After awhile you will begin to notice that little things start to show up. The right baby-sitter, a check in the mail you'd forgotten was coming, a word of acknowledgment from a friend that renews your faith in yourself. Learning to ask for help and being open to receiving it are two of the most essential survival skills I know of for the first-time mom over forty.

A History of Rejection and Disappointment

Lois chose domestic adoption at forty-five without ever having had the desire to bear children herself. "When I was younger, I always thought I'd adopt," she said. "I believed that bringing a child into the world was a ridiculous thing to do. There are just too many people on the planet, and I never really wanted a little being just like me. Besides, I was never very interested in babies—they seemed to be all fluids. I was more interested in kids who could already talk."

Lois began a career as a political activist at age twenty. Twenty-five years later, she was feeling burned out and disillusioned with the possibility of creating genuine social change. For years she had filled her life with children who weren't her own. She had been a foster parent to abused and throwaway kids since she was twenty, and had helped raise the daughter of her now ex-partner for eleven years. Lois sat in my office as we talked. At forty-seven she was still blessed with naturally curly red hair and fair white skin. She told me that by the time she was forty-four she was "totally bored with my career, parties, people; totally bored with the enormous social opportunities that awaited me; bored with art, bored with literature." At forty-four she suddenly found herself wanting her own child. "At first I dismissed it and said, 'Oh my God, Lois, you're watching too much TV. The propaganda is getting to you.' But the desire persisted. It felt like a hormonal takeover."

Lois met with a social worker and laid out her life situation. "She knew I was single, she knew I was a lesbian, she knew I wasn't willing to take on a hopeless cause. She showed me many children, and it was devastating to realize how damaged most of them were."

We brought my son home from India when he was fifteen months old and weighed only fifteen pounds. I had read all these books about the toys infants need to develop coordination and about parents who spoke Portuguese to their babies when they were still in the womb. I was terrified my son would go through life with a permanent disadvantage because he never had any of these things in the orphanage. But he's three now, with highly advanced language and motor skills. It helps to remember how incredibly resilient children really are.

SUSAN, FORTY-SIX-YEAR-OLD MOTHER OF THREE-YEAR-OLD STEPHAN

Lois was matched with her son, David, two years ago when she was forty-five and he was five. "David had a history of rejection and disappointment; he had been trying to sell himself to various adoptive parents since he was three," Lois said. "When he first arrived, he slept with me, and every night he tied my wrist to his wrist with a little string. His mom left him places for up to six months at a time, and each time, she'd depart while he was sleeping. If I ever untied the string to go pee, David would wake up and say, 'You left me.' He'd feel totally betrayed."

Becoming David's mother has marked the end of a depression that had been creeping up on Lois as she tried to envision a childless future, but she also admits that nothing in her experience as a foster parent prepared her for David's constant need for attention and reassurance. "All the energy I used to put into political causes goes to him now," she said. "Some of my friends understand, but others have drifted away. They don't realize what a full-time commitment motherhood is—they don't understand that I can't spontaneously go out anymore, or they think what I'm doing is boring."

It is not unusual to hear older first-time moms comment on friendships that did not survive the arrival of a child, especially an older child with a high level of need. Cultivating new contacts often means seeking out other families with whom you can share practical and emotional support. If you are single, consider contacting Single Mothers by Choice or Parents without Partners (see Resources, page 198), or any other local single parent network. Some of these groups organize playgroups and childcare co-ops, which will not only widen your social circle, but will give you the time you need to tend to yourself and to return to parenting filled with more grace and less grit.

She Lost the Only Life She Had Known

Tracy is a "DES" daughter. Her mother took DES—diethyl-stilbestrol—when Tracy was in utero. This powerful synthetic estrogen was prescribed to three to six million American women between 1941 and 1971 in the mistaken belief that it would prevent miscarriage, despite the fact that studies showed conclusively as early as 1953 that it was ineffective. DES crosses the placenta and damages the reproductive system of the developing fetus.

Tracy is now forty-eight and has been a high school teacher for the past twenty years. She spoke freely at a Wednesday night support group about the cause of her infertility.

"I had four miscarriages in my late thirties and early forties because of the DES. Everything was pointing to not trying again. At the time, I was in a relationship with a man whose wife had died and left him with two little girls to raise, and when things didn't work out between us, I noticed that what I really missed was the parenting relationship. That winter my mother went in for open-heart surgery and died unexpectedly during the operation. It was a very hard time for me; I felt incredibly sad and alone. I thought for a long time about what to do with the money she had left me, and I decided that I wanted to adopt a child. I had lived in South America for several years and I speak Spanish. My dad had lived in Peru and is also bilingual. I knew my extended family would be very supportive of a Latin American adoption, so I started the paperwork and got a referral to Honduras a year later. It's one of the countries open to single adults over forty.

Sometimes our family seems very small. I've certainly toyed with adopting a second, and if I had done this five years earlier, I probably would have. But I like our small family. Katie's never really asked for a sibling. Instead we added two cats to our family, and recently two goldfish. It works well. We're very close.

PAULA, FORTY-FOUR-YEAR-OLD MOTHER OF THREE-YEAR-OLD KATIE

"I met my daughter, Anna, when she was four months old," Tracy went on. "I stayed in Honduras for the month of January and then went home, planning on coming back for her in April when the paperwork was complete. But in March, Honduras closed adoptions, and the agency I had been working through was put out of business for irregularities. Then the lawyer lost contact with the birth mother and had to go to court for an abandonment decree. All this time I had been sending money so that Anna could stay with the same foster family she'd been with since she was born. By the time I was allowed to go get her, she was two and a half years old and had been with them the whole time. The family loved her like a daughter, and Anna of course thought they *were* her family. I explained to them that although youth wasn't something I could offer Anna, my family was very close knit, and they were all eager and ready to love her.

"Leaving was very traumatic for all of them," Tracy said. "Her foster mother cried the whole night before we were scheduled to leave. And Anna lost the only life she had known. She left her language, her country, her family, and found herself on an airplane with me coming to the United States. I kept wondering if I was doing the right thing for her. Would she be better off if I left her with her foster mother? And how would the foster family manage once I stopped sending money? After we were home for a few weeks, I showed her the pictures I had taken of her in Honduras. When she saw the picture of her foster mother, she dissolved into the deepest grief I have ever seen a toddler go into.

"Losing her foster mother has never stopped affecting our relationship," Tracy continued. "Anna is eleven now, and she still has ambivalent feelings. On the one hand, she really loves me, and on the other hand, on some unconscious level she believes I stole her from her family. When she was in first grade, I took her to a therapist because she was so angry. She did this elaborate play fantasy with all these baby animals in the zoo. She said someone came and stole them because they were 'so cute.'

"I could really use a village to help raise this child," Tracy said softly. "I have no regrets, but sometimes I get depressed and worry that we will never have a normal mother-child relationship. I have never had to call upon such reserves of patience, fortitude, and love, and sometimes I feel greatly in need of more personal time and space. When people ask me about adoption I say, "If you only want to hear the positive, I'm not the one to talk to.' You really need to feel like, 'Motherhood is my path, and my life won't be complete without it. I don't care how difficult it is or what special needs my child might have, I'm going ahead with it.' If you have that attitude, go for it."

Tracy and her daughter share a deep and difficult bond, and both struggle in their own ways to resolve issues of ambivalence. It will be years before Anna can look back on her beginnings in a foster family with an adult's perspective and assess what growing up in poverty in Honduras might have meant to her. In the meantime, Tracy has created support for herself by getting together with other parents who have adopted children from Latin America, a group she was put in touch with by Latin American Adoptive Families (LAAF). RESOLVE, Inc., a national organization with chapters in most cities, is another group that offers support for individuals and couples in all stages of infertility, adoption, and parenting after infertility. These

> On my birthday, my friend asked me, "If you could meet three people in the world, who would they be?" The first one would be my son's birth mother in Calcutta. I feel responsible to her. I'd want to tell her that he's fine. That he's brilliant. I'd want to see the pieces of him that are from her.
>
> APRIL, FORTY-EIGHT-YEAR-OLD MOTHER OF SIX-YEAR-OLD ARI

groups, as well as Families for Russian and Ukrainian Adoption (FRUA), Families with Children from China (FCC), and the National Adoption Information Clearinghouse (NAIC) will all send you a list of adoption support groups in your state (see Resources, pages 191–92). Organizations like these provide not only the opportunity for parents to meet and support each other, but also a way for their children to stay connected to and proud of their culture and country of origin.

Just Getting Started

Lynn's decision not to have children grew out of the power inequities she had witnessed between her parents. Determined not to end up in the "undervalued role of mother," she had two abortions in her twenties and went on to become a successful computer programmer for the next two decades.

"There was just too much breeding going on out there and why anyone would go to great lengths to do it was beyond me." Lynn told the support group. She went on to say that she was "a happy childless person" until she married her husband when she was forty-four. "One of his conditions was having kids, but I was starting menopause and refused to go the fertility route. I wouldn't even take my temperature. Fortunately he didn't need to have his genes replicated, so we adopted our son from an orphanage in South America." Now five years later, Lynn says, "It's like we've always been together. Not having had a birth child I can't say for sure, but it seems like there's no way you could love a birth child more. Being a mother to Miguel is more rewarding than I thought it would be. I wasn't aware of the love and protection I'd feel. All those years I modeled myself after men because they seemed to have the power, but now what I'm experiencing with my son is what they missed out on: the intimacy of relating."

Lynn's son, Miguel, was diagnosed with developmental delays once he started school, but Lynn expected that. "He had no trouble picking up conversational English in three to six months, but Miguel had never been read to and hadn't spent much time outdoors. He didn't know words for basic feelings in his first language, so when we started talking about ideas and feelings in English he didn't get it, because he didn't have the concept in his first language. He didn't have words for certain kinds of foods or clothing. He didn't know what a vacation was. There just wasn't a whole lot of learning going on in the orphanage," she said.

Original language loss and new language development may take longer for an older child, especially one who has been abandoned or institutionalized. But instead of labeling them "slow," their developmental needs are better served when educators and parents see these children as just getting started. Communication is a learned skill, and fortunately one of the gifts many first-time older parents have to offer their children is the time and inclination to communicate.

There's No Such Thing as a Grateful Orphan

Jean was one of the older mothers in our Wednesday night support group. She had adopted her first child when she was forty-eight, her second when she was fifty, and was now one week shy of her fifty-fifth birthday. "That puts me in child-bearing age during the Vietnam War," she said. "I married a conscientious objector and we moved ten times in ten years. Things were so uncertain that I didn't feel it was fair to have any children. Then I was divorced for ten years, so I didn't have any children because I was single. I got my music teacher's certificate and got married again when I was forty-four. My husband was six years older than I was and reluctantly agreed to have children." Jean tried unsuccessfully to conceive for several years before she found out that the Dalkon Shield, which she had used as contraception for two weeks in her twenties, had caused her infertility. The Shield was marketed in this country from 1971 to 1974, and during that time was implicated in a high number of cases of pelvic inflammatory disease, the cause of Jean's infertility. It was taken off the market in the United States in 1975 but continues to be distributed abroad.

"By the time I figured all that out, I was forty-seven years old and had symptoms of the onset of menopause. By then my husband said, 'No children, no way, no how . . . you'll just have to get over it.' But children are my top priority in the world. I teach children, and some days I'd be so filled with grief over not having my own I could barely make it through the lessons. There would be older adopted kids in my class and I'd say, 'There are kids out there who need homes . . . where are mine?'"

Jean paused and then went on. "I went into therapy to get over this idea that I would have children. I kept telling myself that you don't always get what you want in your life, you just miss out sometimes. I went back to school and got a master's degree in education to keep busy. One night my husband was watching a news program about the arrival of the first adopted Russian children to come to our city, and I burst into tears. It was as if none of the therapy meant anything, school meant nothing to me. I was like a woman possessed, crying, 'My children are in Russia! I've got to get to them!' I told my husband he could sign divorce papers or adoption papers; I was going to do it with or without him." Jean and her husband did divorce—raising children had never been his desire.

During the next five years, Jean traveled to Russia twice to adopt two young girls who had been institutionalized their entire lives. Jenna, age ten, had worked for the orphanage on a collective farm and because of her strength had been used as a "farm animal." Misha, age seven, had been raised in an orphanage with caregivers who had provided more nurturing and had been better prepared for "export."

"Misha had better social skills than her sister-to-be, but she still wet her bed and could barely walk," Jean said. "Neither of the girls knew how to use eating utensils because they had never been taught. Jenna had been emotionally and sexually abused by women in the orphanage, and for the first two years she was holy hell on wheels. She didn't want a mom at all and wouldn't let me touch her. Misha was a child who wanted a mother, so over time Jenna saw that she could get close to me without getting hurt. It's a good thing I wasn't expecting the Gerber Baby," she said.

"During that time I gave up getting affection from Jenna," Jean continued. "I finally had to decide that it was okay for her not to like me. Instead I focused on giving her the things she needed to make it on her own when she was grown up. You don't take a ten-year-old out of her country, culture, away from everything she knew, for her to fail in this country. In Russia, she would have been out on the street at sixteen and probably would have become a prostitute. When she fought me and said she wanted to go 'back home,' I would say, 'They didn't have enough food for you, there were too many kids in the orphanage. All I'm doing is giving you the food, the medical care, the education you need so that you can grow up strong and healthy and take care of yourself. When you're older if you need to go back to Russia, that's fine with me.'"

Jean talked further about the slow, arduous bonding process with her children. "It's taken years for us to learn to love and trust each other," she said quietly. "They didn't love me at first. Why would they? They didn't even know me. I kept thinking that over time, 'If I do what I say I will do—cook the meals, provide health care, education, the basic maintenance, day after day, these children will come to trust me. If I am consistent and can be depended upon, they will eventually begin to lean into me.'"

During her first year with Jenna, Jean relied heavily on the support and insights she received as part of group training at the adoption agency. The trainer suggested that each prospective parent imagine herself or himself a ten-year-old from America on a plane, going to live in a thatched hut in a Masai village. "You're going to live with a wonderful family in this village," the trainer had continued. "They're going to put bones in your nose and stretch your neck with brass rings. Your breakfast will be blood from slaughtered cattle mixed with fresh milk." Then she asked the prospective parents what they were feeling. Several people croaked, "Terrified." "That's right," she commended them. "The child is terrified. She didn't ask for any of this. It doesn't matter how much you're giving her. You've changed her language, her culture, her religion, her food, and her friends—everything that's been known to her. No matter how hard her life was before, it was familiar to her; it was home. Some 'behave' better than others, but nonetheless they're traumatized. Try to remember," she concluded, "there's no such thing as a grateful orphan." Jean says this awareness helped get her through the years when her kids were freaking out. "Yup, I'd say to myself," she laughed, "They're in that little mud hut and I'm trying to put brass rings on their necks and I expect them to be grateful."

Jean told us that one of the ongoing issues for her continues to be expecting gratitude from her children for all she's given them. This expectation is, of course, a common pitfall for all parents, but especially so for older parents who adopt with hearts so full of hope and expectation. Jean is certain that she couldn't have survived the last five years if she had been a younger parent. "I didn't have enough in my emotional bank account to handle these kinds of kids when I was younger," she said. "I wasn't full enough as an individual to withstand not receiving love from them for so long. It's like giving a constant transfusion. You better know how to replenish your own blood supply because it may be a one-way street for a long time."

While it's a cliché that our children aren't here to fulfill our needs and expectations, it's a cliché worth revisiting. Adopted children come from a place we may never fully know. But in truth even our biological children are mysteries to us when they arrive. One of the great gifts midlife mothers bring to parenting is the maturity to see their children for who they really are, apart from their expectations. Having waited longer to become parents, these women often feel a fundamental satisfaction with their lives and their accomplishments, which translates into needing less emotional gratification from their children. Many mothers who have adopted report the surprise and delight they feel when they let go of their cherished notions of who their child "should" be and instead witness the blossoming of their child's own unique personality. Moreover, our children, who are never who we thought or maybe even hoped they'd

One of my biggest issues with my mother was that her expectations of me had to do with all the stuff *she* didn't accomplish in her lifetime. As an older mother, I know who I am and what I like to do. I have my own identity and my daughter can have hers.

LINDA, FORTY-THREE-YEAR-OLD MOTHER OF ELEVEN-MONTH-OLD DIXIE be, most often embody exactly the qualities *we* need to grow and develop into *our* highest potential. And for this gift that our children bring, we too may be grateful.

Meeting Your Destiny

It seems fitting that adoption, which may have begun with legalities and bureaucracies, should end with the people fate meant to be together at long last finding each other.

Kirsten decided to stop trying to conceive and to begin considering adoption after several years of emotionally devastating and ultimately unsuccessful infertility treatments. Shortly after she made this decision, she dreamed one night that she had given birth to a beautiful baby boy. She loved this newborn with all her heart; upon awakening tears of maternal joy streamed out of her eyes as she remembered the dream. So struck by the tenderness of the connection she had felt with this infant, she recorded and dated the dream in her journal. Kirsten spent the next two years saving money and then jumping through the necessary bureaucratic hoops to adopt a son from India. When she met him, she discovered that he had been born the same night she had her dream.

As a forty-four-year-old two-time cancer survivor, Wendy longed for motherhood and pursued it passionately for years before she finally met up with her destiny. The morning I called her at her home in Santa Cruz, California, she was playing in bed with her three-year-old daughter, Ella. All during our interview I could hear Ella singing and talking to herself, a delightful, happy sound. Wendy was diagnosed with cancer when she was twenty-six and underwent chemotherapy and radiation. A few months after the treatments were complete, she unexpectedly became pregnant. "I knew that being a mom was something that I wanted, but I felt too vulnerable physically. I wasn't employed—the cancer had completely stopped me in my tracks. The doctors said that they'd rather I didn't choose pregnancy because they couldn't really follow me that closely with X rays during the next the two years when they needed to track my recovery. So after much writhing around, I finally decided to have an abortion. I kept thinking about having kids, but the time wasn't right. But then at thirty-four, I was diagnosed with breast cancer. It was the direct result of the radiation treatments on my chest. This second round of chemo put me into early menopause. I was very clear by then that I wanted to be a mom and adoption always felt like an option; I just had to take it one step at a time in terms of processing what was happening to my own body. It took a couple of years until it was pretty certain that I was going to live and be cancer free. During that time my partner Sam and I fought a lot—he was afraid childbirth might do me in, and he didn't want to be a single parent if I should die. Adoption took away the risk and assuaged his fears about me and my body."

> Parents learn a lot from their children about coping with life.
>
> MURIEL SPARK

Wendy heard, through a midwife, of a young woman who wanted to put her baby up for adoption. Wendy's excitement grew until the last minute when the young woman chose to give her baby to someone else who could afford to pay her a large sum of money. It was a huge disappointment, and Wendy grieved deeply.

Wendy turned to her extensive network of friends for support. "They did a letter-writing campaign to raise money for an international adoption," she said, "and at nine every night they all pictured me with a baby. It was really important for me to imagine that possibility. Once I started the paperwork toward adopting a child from China, there was an outpouring of support. People started sending us money—his family, my family, and our friends. When it was time to go to China to get our daughter, I realized that I wanted to go alone. Sam understood. It was something I had longed for so long that it felt like I needed to do it by myself."

Wendy went to China with a group and a translator. The only information she had received about her daughter was her Chinese name and her weight. "I knew she was in good health, but I had never seen a picture of her. At the orphanage, the director came and talked to us. She told us that they considered themselves the 'aunties' to these babies. She told us at length how to take care of them, which I really liked. They had a lot of love and compassion for these kids. The other members of the group had heard the short version of my life—we had told each other our stories in the long van ride going to the orphanage—so everybody was glad to let me go first. The doors opened and the director came in with one of her aides carrying my daughter. They placed her in my arms and everyone just cheered. You could feel a palpable scintillation in the room, like everything was sparkly lights. It was one of those incredible moments in your life when you are walking into your destiny. There was something about the two of us coming together that felt like it was so big, so right, and supposed to be. It was something I had worked toward since 1983 when I had my abortion."

Wendy returned home to find her partner Sam "falling over himself with happiness at the airport. He was a protector there to take care of us. He brought tea in a thermos, and

When Emma came from Russia she was fourteen months old and weighed only fourteen pounds. Very malnourished. Very tiny. But I didn't notice. She was beautiful, and I was her mommy. We bonded immediately. I fell in love in an instant. And I've never looked back. Motherhood is everything I thought it would be and more. It's amazing to me that my love for Emma keeps growing. How is that possible? I don't know, but it is. Emma is now seven and a beautiful young girl.

JENNIFER, FORTY-NINE-YEAR-OLD MOTHER OF SEVEN-YEAR-OLD EMMA

chocolates, and an ice chest filled with goodies. I was in a daze. Ella and I had been on a twenty-four-hour journey. I was in bliss but exhausted. Sam scooped us up and got us home. He had candles and flowers waiting for us. It was a few days after Christmas.

"Life is rich now," Wendy said in her deep, soft voice. "I'm more aware of my mortality on a day-to-day basis because of what I've gone through. It makes my time with my family so precious. I wish I had more energy, I wish I had more time ahead of me. Hopefully we'll have a lot of time together, but who knows? I'm just going to enjoy it now."

Not knowing where the road leads doesn't always mean we're lost. Women who grieve the loss of a biological child and then move forward to embrace adoption often describe being led into a process that deepened their hearts as they marveled at the multiple ways love was waiting to be found. Deciding to adopt a child requires developing resources, internally as well as externally, to meet challenges that may not have been expected or invited. It means cultivating the awareness that there is goodness and purpose in the universe, and that we are not meant to struggle alone. It means learning to ask for help, and recognizing it when it arrives. It means honoring our deepest passion to be a mother, and trusting that the winding road home will lead us there.

The Journey Book

HIGH HOPES AND GREAT EXPECTATIONS
When you have the time, make a list or write a paragraph that speaks to all the high hopes and expectations you had for the

child you were preparing to adopt. Did you imagine harmony and easy times? Did you picture a child who would willingly soak up all the years of accumulated wisdom you were eager to impart? Did you imagine that your child would be forthcoming with expressions of love and gratitude?

Now make a list, write a poem, or fashion a collage that illuminates the many ways your child has grown and continues to grow into his or her own unique individuality. What are his talents? What does she find joy in? What hobbies or interests are completely different from your own?

Finally, write about the woman you have become *because of,* not *in spite of,* these expectations not being met. Has your heart deepened in its capacity to feel compassion for yourself and others? Has your awareness grown to include gifts and talents in your friends and family you might not have recognized before? Has your love been stretched and tested in the fire in ways you could never have imagined? Describe the greatest gift your child has ever given you.

CREATING SUPPORT

Write for five minutes nonstop about what sustains and replenishes you physically, emotionally, and spiritually apart from your relationship with your child. Some items may recharge you in two hours, like a bubble bath or a movie by yourself, while some will require more time and money, like a trip to Tahiti. Make a list of all the members of your extended family or support group who could spell you at least once a week so that you can restore and renew yourself.

PROCESS ART: REMEMBERING WHAT REALLY MATTERS

The following exercise is contributed by Wendy Trayberg, two-time cancer survivor and mother of Ella.

Wendy has developed a program called "Art For Healing" that she now directs at Stanford University Hospital where she engages patients, family, and even staff in making art that expresses their experiences. She also offers "Art For Healing" in individual and group sessions especially for mothers wanting to use process art as a means of self-expression and renewal.

"It was during my first diagnosis and treatments for cancer that I discovered process art. Later I continued to make process art for myself. The subject was my longing to be a parent and my journey to adopt my daughter. I did copious drawings, paintings, and collages. Creating images as I was feeling them, not worrying about them being 'pretty,' recognizable, or finished 'gallery art' helped me to find my feet and stay on them.

"Now that I am a forty-four-year-old woman, two-time cancer survivor, and mother of an almost four-year-old daughter, I continue to make process art for myself. I create art not to lose myself but to remember what really matters: to keep myself grounded so that I am as present as I can possibly be. I want to relish this gift of my life and the blessing of motherhood that I have been given.

"I use the art as a way to just be with myself, to tell the truth of how I am feeling. My anger, my fears, my grief, my hopes, and my dreams. What is wonderful about process art is that it helps me go deeper, not so much to change how I feel but to express it fully. And that brings me back to myself. Back to my own preciousness, back to the miracle of my daughter. Back in harmony with myself and with her.

"One morning I woke up feeling anxious and depressed. Ella was grumpy too, and then I got a migraine headache. We had breakfast. I had tea and ibuprofen and *still* felt like I had an elephant sitting on my head. In my miserable state, a little light went off: 'Let's make process art, Ella.' We set up her easel with each of us on opposite sides with big paper and brushes and pie-pan palettes with every color of tempera paint we had. We had a wonderful time slathering on paint, both of us making big messy creations. Ella became relaxed and happy, and my migraine melted away.

"Here's how you can do process art: Find a time and space where you won't be interrupted. Choose paper and art materials that delight you and speak to you—watercolors, finger paints, temperas, chalk, oil pastels, crayons, clay, colored pencils, or anything else you may want to use. Choose a color you feel drawn to and make any motion on the paper you want. Let it reflect how you feel *right now* in this moment. You may close your eyes or use your nondominant hand. You can listen to music while you make your art.

"If you had no words to express anger, sorrow, loss, joy, hope, what would your art look like? You can notice the critical voices, but you don't have to believe them. You can even draw them. Listen to yourself deeply. Play! Create an internal self-portrait that expresses who you are and how you are feeling in this moment.

"This is a simple and age-old process that makes art from our lives. It's a potent way to remember ourselves, our children, and our connection to all that is. Sometimes we get scared and think we don't know how, so be soft with yourself. Give yourself permission to be a beginner."

For more information, you can contact Wendy Trayberg at 343 Dufour Street, Santa Cruz, CA 95060. Or leave voicemail at (650) 725-8915.

CHAPTER SIX

The Sandwich Generation

I used to wear this "I'm just fine" mask, sort of my public
face, but the experience of caring for my mother and
caring for my family, not to mention working full time, has
definitely changed me. I don't try to hide my vulnerability
from the world anymore.

PHYLLIS, FORTY-EIGHT-YEAR-OLD MOTHER
OF SIX-YEAR-OLD TWINS, JEWEL AND ABRAHAM

I grew up around the corner from my grandmother. The distance was one I could travel safely alone, and I did, almost
every day of my life from the time I could navigate the block
between us until I left for college at age seventeen. My grandmother had escaped the pogroms of Russia at the turn of the
century and arrived in New York City at sixteen to work in a
cigar factory until her elder brother arranged her marriage to
a stranger. She never lost her peasant ways, and her earthi-
ness was the perfect antidote to my mother's fastidious housekeeping and perpetual striving to assimilate into the upwardly
mobile American middle class. When my mother would not
allow me to have pets because of their "messes," it was my
grandmother who made her garage available for the stray cats
I adored. I biked over for my allowance, which she gave freely.

I biked over for hard candies, to visit my cats, and to help her pickle green tomatoes in her basement. I biked over to bask in the unconditional love she offered and to escape the confusion and pain that awaited me at home.

I left the East Coast when I was twenty-five. By then, my grandmother was old and frail, and living in a nursing home. On our last day together, I took a photo of her that is still on my desk, and when I stooped to kiss her good-bye, we both knew I wouldn't see her again. We kept in touch by telephone, but it was never a very satisfying communication. She died when I was twenty-seven. Before she was buried, my brother removed her wedding band and sent it to me, thousands of miles away, and I have worn it ever since.

In sharp contrast, my relationship with my mother was never easy. Over the years, time, distance, and some good therapy have healed many of the wounds, but nothing motivated me more to seek reconciliation with her than the birth of my daughter. I wanted desperately for my little one to have a "grandma," someone with whom she could experience the magic I had known as a child, someone she could turn to for love and understanding when our bonds strained, someone, in all honesty, I could leave her with overnight while I slipped out the back with her daddy. Reading about the Chinese custom of burying alternating generations—grandparent and grandchild—together in recognition of their natural affinity only supported my desire to facilitate their relationship. But at the time my daughter was born, I was living six thousand miles away from my mother. Three years later the distance was a manageable two thousand miles, but still not what you'd call living around the block. My mother had already "played" grandmother to my brother's kids, who were now grown: she'd done the zoo, the weekend baby-sitting, the childproofing of her home, and the feeding pigeons in the park. By the time my daughter was born, she had outlived two husbands and now preferred spending her time getting to know her third.

We made a point to visit back and forth twice a year, but each time she was a stranger to my daughter, certainly no one I could consider leaving her with overnight. My daughter was eight when my mother's husband died. It was a great loss to my mother practically as well as emotionally, since she had been suffering from the progressive loss of her sight to macular degeneration. She had depended on him to help her with a million things big and small that she couldn't do for herself. When she determined that she could no longer see well enough to drive, my brother, mother, and I made the decision to move her to a local retirement community, which provided transportation, socializing, and a medical staff, should she need one.

Her new home was significantly smaller than the one she had been living in for the past twenty years, and so my brother and I spent two weeks going through the possessions she had gathered over six decades. We made piles to be discarded, donated, moved to her new home, and shipped to my home so that I might become the keeper of her memories. Each night, tired and emotionally drained, I called home to find out how my husband and daughter were managing. Had Sasha finished her science project? Was she brushing her teeth like the dentist showed her? Was she being nice to her daddy and helping him around the house? Not only did I mourn my daughter's loss of a grandma, I realized I was now officially a member of the "Sandwich Generation": baby boomers who have postponed parenthood until midlife and who now, as adult children, find themselves responsible for the care of their elderly parents as well as for their young children who are still living at home.

The profile of the typical sandwich generation member is female, forty-five years old, partnered, raising a family, and working either full or part time. By midlife, these women have managed to strike a workable, if precarious balance between home life, significant relationships (hopefully with herself as well as others), and career. But when caring for aging parents—local or long distance—gets added to the balancing act, there may finally be more balls in the air than she knows how to juggle. Women in this situation come to support group struggling with the feelings that are typical, in varying degrees, to caregivers: isolation, loss, sadness, resentment, frustration, exasperation, helplessness, and anger. Many of them have a great deal of difficulty acknowledging the vulnerability and confusion they feel because they have worn their Superwoman mask for so long. Often they have cultivated an "everything's just fine" stance since early childhood. Now they don't know how to ask for help, yet they admit feeling nearly crushed by the weight of additional responsibilities. One group member confessed, "Before, I was dealing with being available for my kid, my partner, my boss, and my friends. I felt like I damn well better be youthful, invigorated, enthusiastic, sexy, efficient, caring, helpful, friendly, cheerful, courteous, and kind. Now I have to be mother to my mother and it is just about overwhelming."

If there are unresolved feelings between adult daughters and their aging parents, the sacrifices required to meet the demands of caregiving will almost always bring these issues to the surface. Even under the best of circumstances, it's common to hear women express sadness because the parents they had hoped they could turn to for support and advice while they raised their children are now themselves in need of support and attention. There's no grandma there to fall back on when the kids are sick, and the years when parents could have been active participating grandparents in the life of her child are now long gone. "I'd never let my son drive alone with my mother," one client said. "Mom drove two thousand miles to Portland to see her sister and by the time she got there all the attachments to the car were gone from her bumping into things."

Being a caregiver to older parents inevitably has an impact on a midlife mother's immediate family. If there was a division of labor in her household, it now needs to be renegotiated as her time and attention get pulled in a new direction, and the steady, predictable help she had to offer children with homework and the daily routines of life can no longer be counted on.

What becomes clear as I work with women caught in this dilemma is that there are wide ranges of conflicting emotions to be reckoned with. Gratitude for a last chance to help a sick or dying parent at the end of their life, frustration that our lives are even more segmented than we ever thought possible. Resentment and compassion. Anger and joy. Pride at watching our kids grow big and strong juxtaposed with the sorrow of watching our parents grow frail and needy. And poignantly, the heartbreak of realizing that with the passing of our parents, we will no longer be someone's child.

> Parents, however old they and we may grow to be, serve among other things to shield us from a sense of our doom. As long as they are around, we can avoid the fact of our mortality; we can still be innocent children.
>
> JANE HOWARD

One night, I invited the women of my support group to bring pictures of their parents and children, and come prepared to talk about their experiences as card-carrying members of the sandwich generation.

Becoming My Mother's Mother

When the mother of our childhood—the mother whose very physical presence meant we were home, whose voice could soothe and encourage, whose style and taste influenced ours no matter how we may have rebelled against it—when this mother needs us to mother her in her old age, it is a new chapter in our lives that poignantly marks the end of an era.

Amy showed us a picture of her and her mother, Rose, taken five years ago when Amy was forty-six and her mom was eighty. Even at that age, Rose looked trim and vital. "Mom lived clear across the country," she began. "Once my daughter was born, it got harder and harder for me to go and visit. My stepdad died four years ago, and I was so absorbed in my own family I really had no idea how depressed and lonely she had become. She certainly wasn't letting on to anybody. We talked on the phone once a week and she always said everything was just fine."

Two years ago, Amy got a call from the hospital in Rose's community. Rose had attempted suicide the night before with alcohol and Tylenol, and had called 911 just before she passed out. The next day, Amy was on a plane to go see her mother.

> Although the world is full of suffering, it is full also of the overcoming of it.
>
> HELEN KELLER

"She was still in the hospital when I arrived, and I hardly recognized her. She looked so scared and alone, it broke my heart," Amy said. "This was the mother who used to take care of me, who sewed my clothes and made matching outfits for my dolls. That mother was gone."

The social worker discussed Rose's heart condition with Amy, something her mother had kept a secret from her, and the fact that it was no longer advisable for Rose to live alone. Amy and her husband, Jack, spent the next month making arrangements to move Rose to an assisted living community a few miles away from their home. "It was my turn to take care of her now," Amy said simply.

But providing care for her mother added new stresses to Amy's family. Jack ran his architectural business out of their home office, while Amy was a stay-at-home mom to their three-year-old daughter, Rachael. If Rachael stayed home while Amy tended to her mother, it meant an interruption of Jack's workday. If Rachael came with Amy, it meant coping with her three-year-old exuberance in a retirement home. "Rachael loved running up and down these big wide corridors," Amy said, "but not all the residents liked the noise or commotion. I was always having to rein her in. I so much wanted Rachael and my mom to get to know each other, but it really was too late. My mom was lethargic and forgetful, and if she asked for a hug or a kiss, Rachael would refuse. There was no way I could protect my mom from that pain and disappointment. She had been such a vital grandma to her other grandkids, but that was years ago.

My father moved in with us when he was eighty and my daughter was ten. For the first year I kept saying, "I just want my life back." Now I say, "This *is* my life." This is what I've been given to do, and I pray every day for the grace to do it well.

LUCY, FIFTY-ONE-YEAR-OLD MOTHER OF ELEVEN-YEAR-OLD JAZZ

"I wanted to do all these nice things for my mom," Amy told the group. "I take her laundry home and bring it back folded and smelling sweet. I take her out to lunch at least twice a week, or out for ice cream, which was always a passion we shared. I helped her get involved in some of the activities they have at the recreation center where she lives, and I usually meet with her medical team once a month. We bring her home to have Sunday dinner with us every week, so that the whole family can be together."

Amy has taken on caring for her mother because, she says, "It feels like pay-back time" for all the nurturing she received as a child. She does it with a full heart, believing that having her mother close to her family will enrich all of their lives. But like many women who suddenly find themselves with the additional responsibility of "mothering" their aging parents, Amy had to renegotiate some of her family's unspoken household rules in order to accommodate her new role. "I had to ask for more support from Jack," she told us. "There were times I simply could not take Rachael with me. He had to rearrange his work schedule to be with her, and it wasn't easy at first. We had our tidy little lives all worked out. These were supposed to be the idyllic years when I stayed home with our daughter, but all that has fallen by the wayside.

"It's not like caring for my mom is a job where I can just call in sick," Amy concluded. "I have to show up. I want to show up."

"Showing up" is an apt metaphor not only for what is required of sandwich generation women as they care for their parents, but also for what they hope is being modeled for their children. One of the ways core family values are transmitted to young children is by having them watch their parents "show up" in times of need. "I hope my daughter is learning that you come through for your family, no matter what," Amy said. By showing up to care for the older generation, many women hope that they are serving as a role model for how they hope their children will eventually nurture and attend to them.

> I have a very simple approach to life. I really believe my job is to just get up in the morning and live my life with as much love as I can muster. We all have to face limitation and loss at some point along the way, so how we go through it is what makes the difference.
>
> BONNIE, FORTY-SIX-YEAR-OLD MOTHER OF FOUR-YEAR-OLD AARON

A Heart Divided

Women who are struggling to meet their responsibilities as parents, partners, and daughters often admit to a nagging sense that none of their roles are being adequately filled. They often describe feeling as if their heart were being torn in two. It seems wrenching and unnatural to have to choose between caring for one's family or one's parents, but that may be exactly what the choice comes down to when geographical distances are involved.

Marla showed us a photo taken of her mother outside the village church on Marla's wedding day, ten years ago. For the last three years, Marla, a forty-eight-year-old English-woman with a six-year-old son, had been flying back and forth to England while her mother was dying.

"I wanted to stay with her, but obviously I couldn't," she said. "Every time I went I had to decide whether or not to take my son. It seemed impossible to take him, but it was just as hard to leave him. I'd spend days before I left writing detailed notes for my husband—remember to cut the crust off Alan's sandwich or he won't eat it, don't let him talk you into junk food for dinner, on and on until I thought I'd lose my mind before I actually got on the plane. A lot of things fell apart for my family at that time. Life was way less organized because I was hugely distracted. Sometimes I considered moving her here to be closer to us, but she had been living in the same community for seven decades—she was rooted and the move wouldn't have been good for her. I thought about moving back home while she was sick, but I couldn't imagine my rambunctious American son surviving in this conservative English village. I patched together home health care for her, and that was the best I could do under the circumstances. I wasn't much good for my son, and I certainly wasn't all I could have been for my mother before she died. It felt like it was my heart that was sandwiched in between all the people that I loved and wanted to take care of. There just wasn't enough of me to go around."

Marla's body sagged in her chair as she spoke. "It was a very lonely time for me. There wasn't any place to process my own needs. My husband was helping out the best he could. And I certainly couldn't arrive in England and say, 'Boy was it a pain in the ass to get here!' I was protecting everyone's feelings, and there was no place to talk about my own."

We all nodded in understanding. Finding ways to take care of her own needs may seem like just one more item on an already impossibly long to-do list for an overextended caregiver. But having a place to express frustration, exhaustion, loneliness, and loss without worrying that your feelings are a burden or a disappointment to someone is essential self-care. Check the Resources section (pages 194–95) for a list of organizations that can connect you to a caregiver group in your area. It's a place to meet and talk with others who are uniquely suited to understand the complexities of what you are feeling without judgment, blame, or shame.

> When we truly care for ourselves, it becomes possible to care far more profoundly about other people. The more alert and sensitive we are to our own needs, the more loving and generous we can be towards others.
>
> EDA LESHAN

Caring for Difficult Parents

The truth is, not all of us had the benefit of being raised by parents who had our best interests at heart. If we were raised by parents who viewed us primarily as a means to fulfill their own physical and emotional needs, the demands of caring for them in their old age can bring up feelings of sadness and resentment—sadness because there is a finality to knowing we will never have the parents we wished for, and resentment because caregiving once again puts us in a position of giving without having our gifts acknowledged or appreciated.

Jade was the youngest of three daughters and had always been her mother's emotional caregiver. But when her father died and her two older sisters moved out, Jade's mother became increasingly more possessive and demanding. The relationship between them became even more complex once Jade herself became a mother of a daughter. When it was Jade's turn to share with the group, she showed us a recent picture taken of her eighty-two-year-old mother and eight-year-old daughter walking together on the beach.

"Oh, how sweet," cooed another group member. "Forget it," said Jade. "It's not like that at all. I can barely tolerate being with the two of them at the same time. My mother gets very jealous when she sees me with my daughter. It kind of flips her out because now there's actually someone else in the world that gets my attention. The day that picture was taken I was running back and forth between her and my daughter making sure neither one of them fell off the cliff. My mom is really needy, like a child, but she keeps insisting she doesn't need anything, which is exactly what my *daughter* says— 'I can do it myself, you don't have to show me, I can open the door myself.' So I'm constantly having to figure out how much I can let each of them do, when they need me, when they don't. I'm constantly checking to see which one is in more danger.

"My mom still lives in the same house she moved into fifty-one years ago, the year I was born," Jade went on. "Her eyesight is failing, and she has no short-term memory left. She rented out the third story to some people I thought could keep an eye on her, but she won't let them. She won't even talk

I know that once my dad is gone, I'll be glad I did everything I could for him, but I'm trying not to sacrifice my own needs while I care for him. He could die tomorrow or in five years. This moment is what counts, and taking care of myself has to be a part of it.

RONA, FORTY-FIVE-YEAR-OLD MOTHER OF TWO-YEAR-OLD KEITH

139

to them. This is her way of letting me know that taking care of her is *my* responsibility."

Every weekend Jade travels to her mother's home, an hour each way, to bring in the firewood, clean out her gutters, answer the mail, and pay her bills. She takes her daughter with her "because she really wants to help out, but it's an added burden for me. Old age has done nothing to soften my mother's possessiveness. She gets down to being about eight years old emotionally, and then she and my daughter fight like two kids who both want my attention. It's bizarre, but there I am, the mediating force between two children. It makes me sad to remember how important it was for me to have a kid before my mother died. I wanted my child to have a grandparent, and I think I wanted my mother to acknowledge me as a grown woman. But she still doesn't see who I am and probably never will."

Jade continues to provide physical and emotional care to her mother, a continuation of the role she was given early in life. In some ways, she is still a young girl trying to make her mother happy, although she knows with the adult part of herself that it's an unlikely outcome.

Seeking to heal old wounds with a parent can be a powerful, sometimes unconscious, motivating factor for an adult caregiver. Sometimes the healing takes place between parent and child as they recognize that time is limited and both grope toward a more encompassing, forgiving view of each other. Sometimes the healing process is a complex emotional journey adult daughters undertake on their own, with the help of a therapist or counselor, or with a circle of good friends. Facing the lonely truth that their parents will most likely never be the nurturing presence they so longed for as a child means finally coming to terms with this loss and disappointment. And while caregiving in the hopes of re-creating a more loving parent may no longer be an option, reconciling losses within oneself often opens the way to new levels of love, which, unbidden and mysterious, have the power to heal old wounds.

Building Community

As the evening darkened and we grew more comfortable sharing our stories with each other, we talked about how our lives had veered from the predictable paths taken by previous generations. The freedom to travel and relocate had been one of the ways our generation distanced ourselves from traditional roles, but it had also meant severing ties with the extended families many of us didn't know we missed until we ourselves became parents. Group members talked with surprise about wishing they lived closer to the families they left behind, and above all, wishing they could call upon the parents they once knew for comfort, support, and advice.

My parents live six hundred miles away. They love my son, but now they're seventy-two and seventy-nine, too old and tired to romp and play. I'm the one caring for my grandmother who is ninety-seven and in a nursing home close to me.

CINDY, FORTY-FIVE-YEAR-OLD MOTHER OF FIVE-YEAR-OLD CHRIS

Several of the mothers described the long distances they lived from their parents as "unnatural," and I was reminded of my recent trip to the pet store. I went to find out why my doves, who had a high rate of success laying eggs and patiently taking turns sitting on them until they hatched, failed to continue feeding their young after twenty-four hours. After losing two baby birds to starvation, my daughter and I had gotten the hang of feeding these tiny featherless creatures with an eye dropper, but I was curious about what seemed to be a lack of maternal and paternal instinct on the part of the parents. "It's different when they live in the wild," my friend the bird expert

141

told me. "There they live communally, and the older birds teach the new parents how to feed their young. Your birds are suffering from the loss of extended family." And while I certainly don't mean to imply that those of us who no longer share in daily contact with our families are lacking in the requisite training necessary to care for our young, it was a poignant metaphor for the loss of extended family and ancestral wisdom experienced by many members of the sandwich generation.

There is no doubt that the absence of active participating grandparents is a huge loss for many women who postponed motherhood and are still engaged in raising young children. The lack of support for a fortysomething mom is a big issue; the lack of that special someone for her child is often even bigger.

"When my son was three or four, he'd go over to my mom's house and they'd bake rolls together, but she hasn't been interested in doing things with him for several years," a client told me. "If he visits her, she cranks up the TV and watches her favorite shows. If my husband and I had wanted her to be a real grandmother, we should have had our little boy twenty years ago. You just don't think, 'Well, if I have my kids younger my parents will be more involved in ten years.' It never even crossed our minds."

Many first-time mothers over forty are seeking creative solutions to fill this "grandparent void." For some women, it means broadening the definition of "family" to include friends and co-workers, or participating in community organizations and activities as a way of forging new relationships. The following are some of the ways the women in my support groups have met this challenge.

Marla asked her older sister, herself a grandmother, if she'd be willing to consider being a "grandma" to her son as well. "You know," she said, "someone who will take the time

142

to impart the morals and ethics I remember getting from my grandparents. Someone who will look like the sun just came out when my boy walks into the room."

Cathleen was particularly close to a woman at work, who was suffering from empty nest syndrome. They worked out a mutually beneficial arrangement, and now Cathleen happily hands her daughter over to her new "auntie" every other Sunday afternoon.

Alex asked her good friends, who had grown children, if they would be willing to become part of her daughter's extended family. For Alex that meant spending time together fishing, hunting, and camping, activities she had enjoyed with her parents who were now too far away and too old to participate.

If none of these options are available to you, consider contacting the Gray Bears (see Resources, page 194) to locate the chapter nearest you. For several decades now, these senior citizens have been redefining old age to include social and political activism. One of these savvy elders just might be the "grandparent" needed to help your child grow into a responsible citizen of the world.

Shadow and Light

Coming to terms with how we feel about our role as caregiver to our parents and to our children is a complex issue, and a woman filling these roles may find that she has strong feelings, without necessarily being able to fully acknowledge or identify them.

Although knowing how and what you feel sounds like it should be a snap, many of us have a hard time naming our feelings, especially when we judge them to be "negative."

Cheerfulness is always considered a plus, anger is usually relegated to the no-no list, and spite and envy are practically cultural taboos. When we try to identify what we're feeling, often there's a little voice that whispers, "You can't feel that! That would mean you're unloving, ungrateful, selfish, and mean. What would people think if they only knew?" For every emotion we struggle to accept, there's a good reason why we "shouldn't" be feeling it. But honestly, isn't it refreshing to be in the company of someone who has gotten over the notion that "perky" is a social asset? And have you ever felt your own heart open in the presence of grief? Getting past the judgments we hold that some emotions are "good" while others are "bad" is not only an essential part of caring for yourself, it's the very essence and wellspring of the compassion and tolerance we have to offer another.

The "Good Enough" Caregiver

When our hearts are being pulled in two or three directions at once, it's hard to recognize that what we are doing for those we love and are responsible for is ultimately "good enough." Many years ago I came across the idea of the "good enough" mother—the mother who was by no means perfect, but who, through her good intentions, provided sufficient love and constancy to raise a healthy child. For midlife women sandwiched in between caring for their families and their aging parents, making peace with limitations means letting go of notions of perfection and honoring the truth that the care they give is their best, and that their best is good enough.

Sometimes what's needed in order to give our best to the people in our care is to free up some of our time by enlisting our family's help with the practical household chores. Kids can participate in these duties at an early age, and it's a tremendous benefit to everyone. My daughter became responsible for doing her own laundry when she was eight years old, and she took enormous pride in her accomplishment. Make a chart of everything that needs doing and divide chores by desire and skill.

If you tend to get really particular about housekeeping as well as mega-efficient and detail-oriented when you're under stress, take a deep breath and decide to let a few things slide. It's almost certain your child would prefer to have you read her a story than to see you clean the bathroom with the time you have to give.

Now is the time for you to banish the Superwoman myth and learn how to ask for help. Caring for your elders is a shared family responsibility; it is not solely the adult daughter's job. Learn to delegate tasks. Discuss strategies for long-term care with other extended family members, including arranging for powers of attorney for financial and health-care decisions, and a living will with instructions regarding life support. Look into options that include assisted living and residential care. Contact your local or state agency on aging to find out about available programs to help you with elder care. With an estimated 25 percent of all households caring for elderly relatives, some innovative companies have begun offering their workers programs that include elder-care benefits, referral services, flexible schedules, and leave policies to accommodate caring for aging relatives. Use the Resources list at the end of this book (pages 194–95) for other suggestions. Find others who are in similar situations, and surround yourself with people who support you in being who you are.

> One of the ways I've learned to make time for myself is by setting a strict bedtime for my son. I read to him, go through the rituals of settling him down, then shut the door and feel a great relief because I know I have at least a couple of hours to myself.
>
> DANA, FORTY-NINE-YEAR-OLD MOTHER OF SIX-YEAR-OLD GABRIEL

There's always something more you could have done, but if you could have done it, you would have. Cultivate the awareness that there's no such thing as perfect, that your best is good enough, and enjoy the opportunity this mercy creates for more genuine heart time with those you love.

Caregiving as a Spiritual Practice

- Caregiving is the opportunity to practice kindness and compassion in action. It offers us the chance to heal old wounds, to let go of grudges, and to accept things as they are right now.

- Caregiving often involves a willingness to change our behavior and reassess our priorities. It confronts us with loss, with our own mortality, and with our need to be helped and supported by others.

- Caregiving challenges us to examine all of our motives and rethink all of our beliefs. Do we believe the myth of "if only"? "If only" we had tried harder, been less selfish, given more, given longer, we could have spared someone we love the experience of suffering?

- Caregiving requires that we tend to our own needs as well as the need of others, and in this sense stretches the boundaries of our kindness to include ourselves.

- Caregiving asks all of this and more, and for that reason can be seen as a spiritual practice. Ultimately, caregiving is about remembering that we are not in control and that life has meaning for all of us, regardless of the outcome.

The Journey Book

SHADOW AND LIGHT

Make a list of everything you are currently feeling and thinking about your life as a member of the sandwich generation. What are you afraid would happen if you allowed yourself the freedom to express your emotions honestly? Write to the heart of your own truth, with openhearted acceptance for your shadow as well as your light. Allow yourself to think the unthinkable thought and to welcome the outlaw feeling.

ASKING FOR HELP

Are you having difficulty admitting that you need help? Do your friends and family think you're invincible? Write about your beliefs concerning independence. What does it mean to you to need and ask for help?

THE "GOOD ENOUGH" CAREGIVER

Write about what it means to you to be a loving person. What does it mean to be "good enough" in the context of your caregiving? If "good enough" isn't good enough, who set the standards you are scrambling to live up to?

CAREGIVING AS A SPIRITUAL PRACTICE

After spending several minutes in silence, write a description of the gifts you have been given at birth that make you uniquely who you are and that you now bring in service to your family and your parents. If you feel there is still more you need to fulfill your tasks, ask for and feel yourself receive these blessings.

Write a prayer or meditation to Spirit that you can read out loud every day. Include thoughts and feelings of gratitude for the bounty you have been given and any prayers you might have for the people in your care.

CHAPTER SEVEN

The Second Batch:
Second-Time Mothers over Forty

My husband is the most emotional person I've ever met.
He can cry at flowers blooming. On our first date, he took
me to the opera and cried his eyes out while I was just trying to follow what they were *saying*. He looked to me like
the right dad for my second child.

LEE, FORTY-FOUR-YEAR-OLD MOTHER OF TWO-YEAR-OLD ROSIE

Despite the fact that I adore being a mother, I've often wondered why a woman in her forties with grown children would
decide to have another baby just at that point in her life when
her time, energy, and resources were hers to reclaim. In the
process of meeting and talking with women who made this
choice to mother a "second batch," I learned that they do so
for a variety of reasons. A woman may have remarried a
younger man who never had kids and wanted them; she
raised her first child as a single mom, always wanted a second
child, and then had the opportunity to fulfill her longing with
a new, willing partner; she divorced and remarried young but
never conceived again until her forties; she and her partner of
many years decided to have a second family once the big kids

were grown; she never remarried but having another child remained a strong desire, so with the help of reproductive technologies she had a midlife baby on her own.

Some women relished the opportunity to slow down and enjoy motherhood with their second child in ways their lives as young, single breadwinners precluded. Some mothers described themselves as more easygoing the second time around, some less. Most all of the women I spoke with were better established financially with their second child, and without exception, all described themselves as noticeably more tired.

For better or for worse, these differences do not go unnoted by older offspring. Some of these "first-batch" children are delighted with the change in their family configuration. Other grown children, noting the differences in upbringing between themselves and their young sibling, express resentment and envy. Younger brother or sister may be getting all the toys, time, and attention mom couldn't afford the first time around, and even more poignantly, may have what a child raised by a single mother didn't: an intact family with two doting parents. Working out these feelings with older children is one of the challenges facing these moms.

> I think that a big difference with my second child is that I have the patience of a saint. But maybe it's just fatigue.
>
> LESLIE, FORTY-THREE-YEAR-OLD MOTHER OF TWO-YEAR-OLD PETER AND EIGHTEEN-YEAR-OLD LUCY

Baby, Baby, Baby

It's fairly typical for a woman who has a second child in her forties to have married and divorced young, and raised her older children on her own. Often she's harbored a longing for another child, and when she begins dating again, a perspective partner's willingness to have a child is a major consideration. When a second marriage offers her the chance to mother again, she is usually eager to say yes. "We got it out on the table on our first date," a client told me. "He knew I wanted another child and I knew he was willing."

I invited four women who had "second-batch" children to an informal gathering at my home. It was a crisp autumn morning, and after we all settled comfortably around the fireplace, the conversation turned to the circumstances that led up to having a second child at midlife.

Norma began by passing around pictures of Max, her twenty-five-year-old son, and Carrie, her three-year-old daughter. "One's in medical school and one's in diapers," she said smiling. At forty-eight, Norma is a petite natural blonde with a lingering Texas accent. She told us that she had raised Max as a single mom from the time he was three and that it had been a very positive experience.

"I had a wonderful career in computer sales with several big national accounts," she said. "I entered the field at a time when women were not in business, so the doors were wide open, and I made a very good income. I was able to travel for work and leave him with my ex, who lived in the same town. I thoroughly enjoyed raising him—it was busy, busy, busy. Social events, his soccer games to go to, a bunch of his friends in the house every weekend. But there was always a part of me that wished I could have a little girl too."

Norma and her current husband, Lyle, had a cordial business relationship for five years before they started dating. She knew that he was fifty years old, recently divorced after twenty-nine years of marriage, and had no children. "One day

I think part of the reason my husband feels so excited about our six-year-old daughter is because he has a daughter the same age he hasn't seen for three years, since his divorce. He's trying to reestablish contact with her now. I'm constantly amazed at how saying yes to the passion I felt about having another child has brought so much healing to our family.

MARTHA, FORTY-EIGHT-YEAR-OLD MOTHER OF SIX-YEAR-OLD DYLAN AND TWENTY-FOUR-YEAR-OLD HEATHER

151

after a business meeting we went out for a drink, and I was bold enough to ask him why he didn't have any children. Every man I had gone out with had either had a vasectomy or already had his kids and didn't even want to think about having more. So I was poking around, qualifying him, like what's the deal? I'm not going to waste any time here if you're not interested in kids because I'm about to turn forty. He said it was his wife who didn't want them, that he would have loved to have had a child. Bingo! Here was a very handsome, sensitive man, and I was not going to let this opportunity pass. We started dating and not very long after that he asked me to marry him. I remember thinking, 'Oh my God, I never thought I'd hear *that* question again,' and of course in my mind I was thinking BABY, BABY, BABY!"

My family thinks I'm crazy because I had a baby with my second husband just days after my son turned twenty-one, but when it comes right down to it, I missed having a little one who needed to be cuddled and mothered.

SUSAN, FORTY-THREE-YEAR-OLD MOTHER OF ONE-YEAR-OLD MIA AND TWENTY-TWO-YEAR-OLD MARSHALL

"I remember that feeling," Mari smiled. A tall, slender fifty-two-year-old woman and mother of three, ages thirty, twenty-six, and twelve, she had raised her two older children on her own. She met her current husband, Karl, when both children were in high school. She waited until the youngest had graduated and then moved in with Karl two weeks later. "When my kids left I didn't think, 'Phew—now I have my life back.' A lot of people said, 'This is great, now you've got your freedom and you can do whatever you want with your life,' and I'd think, 'What *do* I want to do?' I had no real desire to go traveling, I didn't have a strong desire to be a career woman. Mothering had always been the most important thing to me, and I wanted to do more of it. I had exactly *three* months without kids in my life before I got pregnant," she grinned. "It wasn't planned, but we knew it would happen. I

152

know the possibility of having another baby was one of the reasons I pursued the relationship. My husband was twenty-eight and I was forty. He was so beautiful and so gentle. I fell in love and all my hormones took over. I'd probably have another child if it weren't for my age."

Lupe helped herself to coffee as she spoke. At forty, she is a grandmother, married to her thirty-six-year-old husband, and mother of their six-month-old daughter. Lupe is the director of a local preschool, which she runs with her twenty-four-year-old daughter Marissa, herself the mother of two small children.

"I was one of those statistic teenage moms," she told us. "I had Marissa when I was sixteen. I lived with her father for a short time, but we were too young to make the marriage work. When I was about six months pregnant, I moved back in with my parents and lived with them until she was two. I had to drop out of high school to care for the baby, so I got my GED at night school." As soon as she graduated, Lupe moved in with an older brother. "My brother helped me get a job, and I found childcare for my daughter. When my daughter was four, she started going to kindergarten, I had my own apartment, and I started taking classes at the local college where I eventually got my master's in early childhood education. It's where I met my husband." I quickly did the math: twenty years ago Lupe was twenty; that would have made her husband-to-be sixteen. "Yes," she laughed. "He lied about his age. He pursued me for two months before I agreed to go out with him.

> I love having babies. The pregnancy is great, birth is great, and watching their growth is great. When I was forty-four, I told the women in my women's group that I was pregnant, and one of them said, "I hope it isn't catching." I realized that she looked extremely matronly, like at forty-four she had gone over the edge and become old, but I didn't feel like I was there yet. I *still* don't feel like I'm there.
>
> REBECCA, FIFTY-ONE-YEAR-OLD MOTHER OF SEVEN-YEAR-OLD MARIE AND THIRTY-YEAR-OLD JAMES

153

"He always wanted kids," she continued, "but it just never happened. I had two miscarriages five years ago, and we were both very disappointed. My husband loves spending time with Marissa's kids, but deep down he wanted one of his own that wouldn't go away at the end of the day. He waited a *long* time for our baby."

So This Is What It's Like

Having a second child in midlife presents a woman with a study in contrasts. She often has more time and money to spend on her second child, while she almost always has less energy. By forty, a woman has usually established the style and rhythm of her life, met many of her personal goals, and satisfied at least some of her worldly ambitions. Priorities have shifted, and what seemed important in her twenties now seems insignificant. "I had more to prove at twenty-three than I do now," one client told me. "I was still trying to find myself." Some women note how little besides mothering really matters to them. Others are surprised to find that they have less, not more, tolerance for disruption. Second marriages may flourish and provide the foundation for a stable family, or they may fail and leave a woman once again parenting on her own.

Several of the women stood to stretch and refill their coffee cups. When they had settled back in their chairs, I asked the group what, if any, differences they had experienced between raising their first children and raising their second.

Norma waited until her son was a sophomore in college to marry Lyle. Seven months later, at forty-five, she was pregnant with her daughter. "I was healthy, I got plenty of rest, and I had stopped working," she said. "I was living in a new place with no friends or family, so it was a whole new world for me after a fifteen-year career with an international company. Once the baby was born, I stayed home and nursed her for a year. It was the most peaceful, joyful time of my whole life. She nursed and slept, cooed, and smiled for the camera. We had a predictable routine of naps, and I'd start supper at the same time every night. I remember looking out my window at a beautiful view of the mountains and I'd think, 'So *this* is what it's like having a baby when you're forty-five.' I don't know of another whole year of my life that was like that, because when my son was born I was twenty-three, and I went back to school to get my master's."

Mari moved closer to the fire and talked about the differences she notices between raising this "batch" and the first. "Someone once said that there are no dress rehearsals in life, but this really *is* one. I get to do it all over again, and I am very glad for the opportunity," she said. "I was so much more relaxed when my youngest was a baby. It was wonderful to be able to just sit down and hold him when he was sleeping instead of putting him down so that I could race around and do all the things I had to do. I take the time to be with him now. I work in his class one morning a week, but I can, because I'm not raising him by myself and I don't have to go and make all the money by myself.

> I was so young when I had my first child. I really had no idea I wouldn't have a second until I was forty-two. Now I know this is the last time for all my baby's "firsts." This is the last first step, the last first tooth, the last time I'll breastfeed. I know how fast time goes by and how fast kids grow up and leave home. I want to be conscious, mindful, and not let a day go by when I'm hurrying my second child to grow up.
>
> MANDY, FORTY-THREE-YEAR-OLD MOTHER OF ONE-YEAR-OLD KYLE AND TWENTY-SIX-YEAR-OLD JUDE

"All the stress and uncertainty I felt as a young parent are gone," she said. "I still have to say no just as many times, but it's easier to do the second time around because I learned from my big kids that there's value in setting limits. We still have the teenage years to get through, but I'm not dreading it like I was the first time. I've lived through zero to eighteen and I know that it *does* resolve itself. I'm having a delightful time with this child, and I think it all goes too fast."

"It *is* really different this time," Lupe said. "When I had my daughter, I was still growing up myself. I knew that in order to succeed I had to get my education, so my whole focus was how to fit my daughter into my plans. Now the focus is how to fit *my* life into what the baby needs. And just sharing this experience is very different. My husband is totally involved and helps out with everything. He watches him during the day when I'm gone, and I watch the baby at night while my husband works a swing shift. Sometimes we're like ships passing in the night, but we're both in seventh heaven. Having a baby is a tremendous responsibility and commitment. When I look back at raising my daughter on my own, I wonder how in the world I did it."

"Doing this alone wasn't something I planned for," Claire said, referring to raising her four-year-old daughter, Skye, on her own. At forty-eight, Claire owns her own electrical contracting business and was the only single mother in the group. Claire's oldest daughter, Ella, from her first marriage, is now twenty-one. "She was just ten years old when I remarried," Claire said. "I wanted another child right away but even back then my husband thought we were too old."

When she was forty-two, Claire unexpectedly conceived. "My husband said he'd support whatever decision I made," she said, "so I decided to have the baby. It turned out to be much harder than I thought it would be. Ella had been kind of a perfect baby, so I thought all babies were like that, but Skye had colic and screamed for the first year of her life. This baby was a dose of another reality. She would cry for hours during

156

the day. I used to be able to drag Ella anywhere and she'd just fall asleep if she was tired, but I couldn't do that with Skye. And there was no one I could leave her with, so I had to figure out how to run the business from home." When Skye was one year old, Claire and her husband separated. "Ella was very helpful during that first horrible year," she said. "But one of the odd things about having an older daughter was that when we were all out together a lot of people thought she was the mother of the baby. Did it bother me? Yeah, sometimes it did."

Claire reflected on the differences between parenting in her twenties and now, again, in her forties. She remembered that when Ella was young, she could go out with her friends until two in the morning and still get up and go to work the next day. "That's out of the question now," she said. "I go to bed at the same time I put Skye to bed. And I'm not as easygoing this time around. I've grown older and gotten more used to my ways. When Ella was young, my life hadn't jelled. Any direction would have been okay, and interruptions weren't a disaster. Now I feel like I have so little time and there are so many things I want to do that I just don't roll with the punches as well."

> If a child is to keep alive his inborn sense of wonder, he needs the companionship of at least one adult who can share it, rediscovering with him the joy, excitement and mystery of the world we live in.
>
> RACHEL CARSON

Claire paused, then added, "But being a mom is still wonderful, despite it all. Skye is a lovely creature. She's very artistic and makes fabulous things. She likes bugs, fossils, animals. She's interested in things I've never even dreamed of. Her passion for living has pointed me in totally new directions."

Claire admits that part of the reason she is having trouble rolling with the punches is because raising Skye on her own has turned out to be more difficult than she ever imagined, and radically different from the relative ease with which she raised

Ella. Skye has recently been diagnosed with learning disabilities, and Claire is now investigating various treatment options. The lack of a partner with whom she could share the joys and burdens of child rearing and decision making was a big loss for her, and unlike the other second-time moms in the room, she was having a harder, not an easier time with her "second-batch" child.

Will You Love This Baby More?

"First-batch" children, no matter what age, inevitably have reactions to the news that a "second batch" is on the way. Some kids are elated. The mother of a fifteen-year-old boy told me that the arrival of his baby brother was a huge relief to him. It meant greater freedom and fewer restrictions because mom had someone else to turn the high beams of her attention on. Some children feel threatened and worry that their mother will love the new baby more. "My daughter really wanted a brother or sister, but she was afraid the baby would be prettier and smarter than her," one second-time mom told me. A forty-four-year-old single woman who decided to use Assisted Reproductive Technology to conceive said that it had been extremely hard for her grown daughter to support her decision. "She's getting married and is looking forward to starting her own family. From her perspective, I'm at a point in life when I should be waiting to become a grandmother and helping her. It's probably embarrassing to her. She doesn't know what to tell her friends or her in-laws." Some grown kids accompany their mom to the doctor's office for sonograms. Some develop close relationships with their new sibling, while some keep their distance. No matter what the circumstance, honoring the feelings of everyone involved is the key to helping older kids come to terms with their new family configuration.

Lupe's daughter Marissa knew that her mom and stepdad had been trying to have a baby for almost twenty years, so she was delighted with the news that they were finally expecting. Lupe also thought that perhaps since Marissa already had children of her own, she felt less competitive with her baby brother, born six months ago.

"She couldn't wait for the baby to be born," Lupe told us. "When we went to register at a store for the baby shower, we completely changed roles. I had no clue what to look for. I was used to being a grandma and buying the girls all kinds of frilly dresses they didn't really need, so I was totally at a loss with a lot of the new stuff on the market. We looked at strollers, and she'd say, 'No, you don't want this one, look at the wheels.' She showed me stuff I had never even *heard* of. It had been a long time since I had bought supplies for a baby. There weren't even disposable diapers back then. I was looking for glass bottles and she said, 'Mom, they don't make those anymore.' And then we just laughed at how ridiculous the situation was."

"My kids had a harder time of it," Mari said. "My twenty-six-year-old daughter says, 'You were never home for *me* after school.' I think she resents watching me take really good care of my twelve-year-old. She wonders if she got taken care of that way. Both older kids hint that I'm overindulging him and think that I'm spoiling him something terrible. But it's so different now.

I was devastated when I found out that a good friend of mine had died unexpectedly of complications from pneumonia. Driving home from the funeral I started thinking that life is very short, with no guarantees of *anything*. I knew then that I needed to go for the dream of having another baby. Whether I got what I wanted wasn't the point. The point was that I needed to try because otherwise I'd always wonder. So I came home and called this clinic I had heard of that was willing to work with women my age, and I started the process.

JANICE, FORTY-NINE-YEAR-OLD MOTHER OF TWO-YEAR-OLD JUSTIN AND TWENTY-SEVEN-YEAR-OLD DENNIS

Now I've got a partner to share the parenting with. By the time my daughter was three, my first husband had split. I was an accountant and pretty much worked their whole upbringing. My son would see his father occasionally to go fishing with him, but my daughter hardly ever saw him. She grew up not having much male interaction. That was the real hardship for her. When she got older, she had to deal with not having male approval and still wanting it. Even in her early adult life she wanted her dad to be there for her, but he couldn't be. She's had to work through not having a picture-perfect family situation, so seeing my new family has been hard on her. But the advantage of being older is that I have the perspective that age brings. I tell her, 'If you think there's any way to cruise through life without some issues to work on, guess again. It's what life has given you. You can bury your head in the sand, or you can make the best of it.'"

Claire told us that even though Ella is now twenty-one and living at college, she still comments all the time on the things that she never had that her sister gets. "Last summer I had a playhouse built for Skye. It was something Ella had always wanted as a kid, and I think she felt bad about her sister getting it. I try to explain that our circumstances were very different when I was raising her by myself, but I know it still bothers her," Claire said. "Back then I was making a lot less money. In fact, we were extremely poor. Ella used to beg to take ballet lessons, but it was out of the question. Even though I'm single again and raising Skye on my own, I can afford lots of things for her that Ella never had."

When I asked Norma about the impact her new family has had on her son, she grew thoughtful. "He's begun to make little digging comments to me about my daughter's life, like, 'Look at *her* Christmas. I don't have any fond memories of

Christmas. She's got it made in the shade because *both* her parents are here.' My daughter is at the age right now that he was when his father and I divorced. In retrospect, I wish someone had encouraged us to talk to a marriage counselor or read a book or *something*. My son always wanted to know why he didn't have two parents like everybody else. Even though we were working so hard to be the best divorced parents in the world, it didn't matter.

"My guilt usually begins around four in the afternoon when I start cooking dinner," she continued. "Here I am, a lady of leisure, and I think back to all those years when I was working and missed dinner so many nights. He's at school a thousand miles away, but I still wish I could call him up and say, 'Hey, I'm fixing your favorite spaghetti— come on by and eat with us.' I'm getting to be the kind of mom with my daughter that I wish I could have been with my son. I think the next time he comes to visit, I want to talk about all of this—his feelings of jealousy, my feelings of guilt—because if we don't, it's going to be like the elephant sitting in the middle of our living room. You can't miss the smell, but nobody wants to talk about it."

When Big Kids Have Little Kid Feelings

My own experience of second-batch families arrived with my husband's teenage daughter, Shauna, who came to live with us the summer she turned fifteen. I had my first and only child a year later, at home, when I was forty-four, and Shauna was there to hold my hand and see her sister born. Over the next three years, she watched her new sibling receive all the devotion and commitment she had not received as a child. She felt shortchanged. It was easy to see the pain in her eyes as she watched her dad take time to be playful and goofy with his new girl in all the ways he had been too preoccupied to be with her when she was that age. This was a dad she had *never* had access to. Feelings of resentment surfaced in Shauna, and she became Queen of the Snide Comment. I slipped into a kind of unconscious guilty response and tried to diffuse her sniping by being extra nice, but it always backfired. We were flailing around in some pretty murky waters until her father and I finally accepted the fact that her feelings were old, deep, and *legitimate,* and that she was *not* going to just snap out of it. We began holding informal family meetings around the dining room table at least once a week—more if the tension began escalating—and what I learned during those years has served me well as I've met and worked with second-batch moms.

When older children start sounding snippy and snide in respect to a new, much younger sibling, I have found that nothing gets to the heart of the matter faster than open, direct communication. It's tempting to take the high moral road and suggest that since they're so much older, and what they are feeling happened so long ago, why don't they let bygones be bygones and get on with things, set a good example, act their age, on and on, until you've spawned a resentment in them the size of New Jersey. But one of the profound truths I have learned from my years of working with people is that if the feelings haven't been processed, they are as current today as they were when they first happened. That means that although your son or daughter may be grown with careers and kids, very much in the swift running current of their own lives, when you go back to talking about issues from their childhood, you may find

> One of the things I've discovered in general about raising kids is that they really don't give a damn if you walked five miles to school. They want to deal with what's happening now.
>
> PATTY DUKE

yourself talking to a very little one who is still holding on to certain memories as if they happened last week. What follows are two highly effective ways to open up communication with a child of any age who is still having feelings about past hurts:

- "I think there are a lot of feelings behind what you just said—why don't we sit down and talk about it?"

- "I made a lot of mistakes—we all do. I expect you to have some resentment, and I'm here to work it out with you."

And then of course, the trick is to open up, listen, not get defensive or judgmental, and not bat back. Your big child may be feeling reluctant to expose these vulnerabilities, so take the time to carefully and completely acknowledge the tender emotions that may be *behind* the content of what they are saying— even if you disagree—before you respond in your own defense. It's a deceptively simple ground rule that brings out the best in everyone.

When it's appropriate, and not just a diversionary tactic, helping the "big kids" remember some of the positive times you've had together when he or she was younger is another effective way to address their feelings of envy and resentment. One forty-three-year-old mom I see in my practice showed her grown son the scrapbooks she had saved, lovingly filled with photos and mementos of the adventures they had taken together when he was young and she was a single mom— skiing, rafting, Disneyland. "The fact that the biggest adventure I currently take with my two-year-old daughter is an afternoon nap hit us both at the same moment and we totally cracked up," she told me. "For the first time he saw something *he* got that she never would."

Second Chances

Less plagued by the worries of first-time mothers, women who have second babies in their forties are, for the most part having a first-rate time. Second children come with second chances: the chance to parent with greater self-assurance and peace, the chance to correct mistakes and right old wrongs. For many, the real gift is the chance to rediscover the magic and wonder of the world we live in a second time, through the eyes of their second child.

The Journey Book

LETTER TO YOUR OLDEST CHILD

In your Journey Book, write a letter to your oldest child (or children) that you may or may not choose to send. If talking in person hasn't been possible, you might want to write an imaginary dialogue that follows the guidelines above for opening up communication around issues of resentment and jealousy. When you feel complete with those issues, describe the experience of having your first child. What are the pleasures you recall, expected and unexpected? What were the gifts you brought to motherhood as a younger woman that you will never again have available to give? Feel the place in your heart where this child lives that is sacred and can never be filled by another. Write about that place in prose or poetry, draw it, sing it, and celebrate it, for there is nothing that can or will ever take the place of the love a mother bears her first-born child.

CHAPTER EIGHT

Out of the Mouths of Babes

My mom always made it clear to me that I was the apple of her eye. She expected me to act older and wiser than the other kids my age and it made me very confident. I consider myself fortunate to have been raised by an older mother, but I also understand that things will be different for me than for most of my friends. They will probably have their mothers around for most of their adult life, and I probably won't.

JOHANNA, TWENTY-THREE-YEAR-OLD DAUGHTER OF
SIXTY-EIGHT-YEAR-OLD JULIA

Last winter I had the flu—the ten-day kind that leaves you looking like that old photo of your mother's mother just before she died. The course of my illness included projectile vomiting, fever, aches, and chills. My head pounded and I moaned a lot. I knew it was just the flu; what I didn't know was that to my daughter it looked like the end of my life. She didn't tell me this directly; instead she confided her deepest fears to Leslie, her best friend's mother. Leslie called several weeks later, glad I was better (read: still alive), and told me how worried my daughter had been about my health. Sasha had assumed that anyone my age who was that sick was *of course* getting ready to die.

The humor of her assumption lasted for a brief moment and was quickly replaced by a stunned sadness as I thought about a young girl brooding about her mother's mortality, an issue most of my contemporaries hadn't even contemplated until their early adulthood. This led me to wonder if other children have concerns about their older parent's mortality that they might be reluctant to share. I started by asking Pamela, a twenty-five-year-old friend, and herself the grown daughter of a first-time mom over forty, if she recalled ever worrying about her parents dying when she was growing up.

"Oh *yes*," she said, "it was always a nagging fear. When I was about seven my father bought two cemetery plots. I remember the salesman coming over to the house and my dad buying them, and me just going into a state, thinking, 'Oh my God, that means they're going to die.' I asked my mom, 'Are you dying?' And she said, 'No. Why?' And I said, 'Because you just bought those things.' She said, 'Oh, that's for the future.' But that didn't make me feel any better. I had more of a sense of their mortality than my friends did with their parents. I remember my mom always talking about not being afraid to die. I think that's important, but I'm not sure she should have talked about it in front of me at such a young age. She would say, 'Don't be afraid to die, it's just a new experience,' and I'd say, 'Are you sure you're not dying?' And she'd say, 'Yeah.' But after that I never wanted to leave home. I was afraid they were going to die and I wanted to be with them all the time."

Pamela grew up in a university town and attended a laboratory school run by the university. When she was eleven, the director approached her parents and asked if they were interested in Pamela being an exchange student in Germany for eighteen months. "My mom asked me if I wanted to go, and I asked her what she wanted. When she said she thought it would be a fabulous experience for me, what I really thought she meant was that she wanted me to go. I thought she wanted to get rid of me because she was old and tired and wanted to be alone with my dad. I hated it there, but I stuck it out. When I came back, I didn't want to leave her again, so I went to college in my hometown so that I could be close to home. I guess I thought if I were with them they wouldn't die."

Curious now if other kids of older parents were holding on to the proverbial beans just waiting for the right place to spill them, I continued my interviews. I asked Roy, the fifteen-year-old son of my friend Maggie, who is a sixty-year-old university professor, if he had concerns about his parents' age.

"My parents are the oldest parents in my crowd," he said, "and sometimes I feel really different. They don't like to go to basketball games like my friends' parents do. And most of my friends have grandparents, but mine are already dead. I guess you could say I'm afraid my parents will die when I'm still pretty young. They just won't be around as long as other kids' parents. They always tell me how healthy they are, but being the child of older parents has made me more aware of the reality of the end of life."

The issues that emerged as I spoke with other children of older parents were ones that were repeated over and over again. On the downside, these kids commented on their mom's declining physical energy, a wider-than-one-generation gap in music and fashion taste, and a tendency to overprotect and micromanage. On the upside, there was a strong positive sense of being very much wanted, which included the benefit of lots of time, attention, and encouragement, and a comfortability in the company of other adults.

The following is a transcript of one of my talks, with ten-year-old Kelly, daughter of my fifty-one-year-old friend Myra.

Myra had spent three years going through grueling infertility treatments before adopting Kelly as a newborn. We set the interview up at a café one beautiful early spring morning. Mom hung around for another fifteen minutes after she said good-bye and then finally left us to talk alone. Very little has been edited out because as you will see it's—like, way cool—in her own voice.

Kelly, do you have friends whose moms are the same age as your mom?
No, they're all younger.
Do you notice any differences?
Yeah, like, one of my best friends' mom is in her early thirties and she's more fun and energetic. She does more stuff with us.
Like what?
Oh, we play games and like that. Like, I play games with my mom, but they're board games. My friend's mom plays tag with us.
So that's a big difference—the energy?
Well, yeah. My mom used to take me to the park to play and she'd run with me, but now she's not like that. Now she says no.
She's more tired now than when you were younger?
Yeah, like the other kids on my soccer team, they have moms who get out there and kick the ball, but my mom just sits there and yells, "Oh bravo!"
My daughter often complains that I care more about what she eats and what she watches on TV than other moms do. Is your mom like that?
Yeah, like, I'll say! We always have to shop at health-food stores. But when I'm at my friend's house we eat slush puppies, we eat candy, we drink Dr Pepper. We get to watch movies, we play Nintendo. Like, almost all my friends have cable or satellite or something, and we don't. My mom says TV is crap. At my friend's house we get to watch anything we want—like *Nightmare on Elm Street*—and her mom, well, she doesn't really *notice*. And if I ask her mom if I can buy a king-size Hershey bar when we're at the video store, she's all, sure, cool, but when I'm with my mom all I can buy is popcorn.

168

So your mom has different standards and taste than the other moms in your crowd?

Yeah, like when we go shopping, she always picks out these oldie-day clothes and I'm, like, "Yeah, that would be nice if I were, like, NINETY." I said, "Mom, I think the only people who would wear that would be from—I don't know—like, thirty years back or something," and she's all, "But honey, it's very nice." And she always wants to rent movies about what happened in the sixties and I'm all, "Mom, trust me, that's going to be boring. It's 2000, Mom." And she's all, "So what?" And I'm all, "Fine, but I'm not going to *watch* it." And she doesn't like any of my music. Like, she always sings these oldie-day songs, or she listens to classical or popular things from a hundred years ago. And when we're driving if she's mad at me she puts in this tape, and this Buddhist guy is talking and he *sucks*. And she's, like, "It's so *calming*." YEEECH.

So you think she's a little behind the times?

Yeah.

Does your mom kind of notice everything you do?

Yeah, like a lot of my friends' moms don't care about their daughters so much. They're like, "Okay, you can go and play," but my mom's like, "Well, let me think about it." She always makes me do homework when all the other kids are free.

She kind of oversees things?

Yeah. She knows about everything. And then, like when I get a bad attitude because I want her to leave me alone, she's all, "No, I'm just going to stay right here," and that makes it worse. If she just left it alone, it would get better.

How would you describe your mom's moods?

Well, one thing that's really scary is that she totally changes sometimes. One time she burned her eyelashes on the stove at home. First she was laughing, and then she started, like, crying because she said I wasn't being very supportive. It's weird. Sometimes she's all nice and then she's, "Grrrrrrh," and it's like, where did *that* come from?

Do you guys do any kind of sports together as a family?

Yeah, kind of. We go skiing. I like to go speeding down and I'll see her on the side of the bunny slope trying to get up and I'm all, "Mom, do you need help?" And she's all, "No dear, I can get up," and then she gets up and she falls right back down. My friend's mom, she's like snowboarding and she's all, "WHEE," and my mom goes down the slow side of the bunny hill and gets down to where it's practically flat and she just falls.

So she doesn't take risks the way a younger mom does?
No. Like my friend's mom, she jumps off rocks, or she'll crazy drive. But like there's this bump in the road on the way home and I say, "Mom, go over it fast," and she's like, "No honey, I'm afraid I'll get dizzy."

Are there any advantages to having an older mom?
Well, one of my best friends, her mom has four kids, and she's like only in her thirties, and she's going to school and, like, she doesn't get *any* attention from her mom. And sometimes when I wake up and come into the kitchen, my mom's already there waiting for me and she's like, "Oh yippy, it's Kelly!" And that makes me feel really good.

I thanked Kelly and told her that when my daughter was seven or eight I started getting really tired, "like, major pooped like your mom." I told her that basically just about everything she was experiencing regarding having an older mom was true—we *are* different. We're more tired; we can sometimes be ridiculously outdated and—gasp—old-fashioned; most of us have only one child so we tend to be overprotective and overcontrolling; we really notice *everything,* whereas younger moms are more, like, *whatever;* and we can really be emotionally unpredictable and crabby. This information seemed to both delight and enlighten her, and when we parted she shook my hand solemnly like an old war buddy.

I knew that my daughter Sasha had feelings about my age because on one of our lap swims—a favorite way of ours to relax and spend time with each other—I asked her, "If there were one thing you could change about me, what would it be?" "Your age," she responded in the blink of an eye. Part of her complaint had to do with what she perceived to be my all-pervasive fatigue, and the issues surfaced again after we saw the movie *Erin Brockovich* together. In the last scene Erin, sitting in her spiffy new office, receives a check for a cool two million dollars for a job well done and prepares to take on her next big challenge. Leaving the movie Sasha was apparently thinking deeply about this display of life force and marveled out loud, "Gee, I thought after she got the money, she'd be tired and not work anymore."

"I'm tired a lot, huh?" I said, going to the heart of the matter. "Yeah," she said. "You just don't do as many things with me as I wish you would."

Sasha asked if I would interview her for this chapter, so on the *Ms.*-inspired Take Your Daughter to Work Day, I loaded up my tape recorder, fresh tapes, and all the courage I could muster, and took my daughter to the local café to interview her on her thoughts and feelings about having an older mother.

I know that your best friend (Mandy) has a younger mom (Leslie). Are there any differences you notice?
Well, sometimes you're tired right after you wake up, and it's like HELLO—that's a really quick day!
It's hard to imagine, isn't it?
Yeah, and you, like, get into your pajamas at 6 P.M.
And Leslie isn't like that?
No, she's more energetic.
What kinds of things does she do with you and Mandy?
Well, she wakes up and she has all these bright ideas for us to do, like, "I thought we should go see a movie today and then on the way home we could stop at the amusement park and then we could go out to eat and then after that we could have a water balloon fight. . . ."
Wow—all in one day?
(We both laugh.)
Yeah, that would be a week for you.

Are there other differences you notice?

Well, she's not so freaked out that I'm going to get poisoned by junk food. You're like, "You can't eat hot lunch at school—it's got chemicals in it!"

So you find me a bit overprotective?

Yeah, you're like, "Oh, my God, I've waited so long for this child, and now I must know exactly how you're doing and where you are and what you've eaten and if you've pooped." You have to know a person's background for two years in order to even let me go to their house. My other friends are like, "I'm going to spend the night at so-and-so's house," and their mom is all, "Okay, be back whenever." Even if I want to go *bike* riding with someone you're like, "Well, I need to meet her parents, and I need to meet her uncle, and I need to meet her cat, and I have to have their phone number, and here's my pager number, and don't wear your sneakers without socks, and take your vitamins, and it's windy, and you have to wear a hat!"

I see. That's pretty clear. So what do you tell your friends about my age?

Well, you're the oldest mother. Megan's mom is the next oldest, she's forty-five. I told them you were forty.

Why did you lie?

What was I supposed to do? They asked me. Mom, remember the *old* guy? (We both laugh remembering a story her friend told her about a fight she had witnessed at the local convenience store between a "*really* old guy, at least fifty, and a young kid.")

What would have happened if you had said I was fifty-five?

I don't know and I don't even want to know. I don't even want to *think* about it.

Do you ever worry that I might not be around when you have children?

It's kind of weird to think about you being dead. It's weird and it's not right because you'd probably make a good grandma.

Do you have other worries?

I worry about, like, when I'm twenty you're going to be sixty-four and that's when I'm going to want to go traveling.

172

Ah, so you're concerned that you'll have to care for a crotchety, decaying old mother just at the time you want to go traveling? Yeah, right.

I see. Well, you don't need to worry about that. I will never ask that of you. I'll find a little house on the beach and go be crotchety next to the ocean.

(We both laugh.)

So, are there any advantages to having an older mom? Well, I like being an only child. I like getting all the attention and not having to share my stuff with a brother or sister. And you and Dad always have the time to help me. And you probably won't get a divorce—you were more experienced when you got married. You don't want to run around and go traveling so much—you stay in one spot. All my friends are moving all around and they keep coming back to our house and going, "Wow, you're still here!" I like that. Even though it can get a little boring sometimes, it's still better.

So that's some of the upside and the downside of having an older mom from a child's perspective. Obviously there's nothing to be done about your age, but there is about your attitude. The following are suggestions for helping you survive the realization that to your kid, you're a geezer, and for helping your kid survive and thrive during those years when she'd much prefer you looked and acted, like, *younger*:

- First of all, kids don't really notice or care about how old their parents are until they are approaching puberty, so if your child is still at that tender age where you are the Magnificent Goddess Who Can Do No Wrong, enjoy it, because it *will* change.

- When your child does begin to notice the differences between you and their friends' thirtysomething moms, take a deep breath and imagine yourself growing a tough lizardlike hide. Your child is developing the brain capacity that allows him or her to measure, evaluate, and discriminate. Unfortunately, you are what's currently under the micro-scope. Most of the time they're actually not trying to be cruel. They are simply honing their observation skills on the nearest stationary object. Take it from me: the less personally you feel about it, the quicker they'll move on to something or someone new. And if it is personal and the intent is to wound, I have found it in everyone's best interests to set healthy boundaries. "The way you're talking to me right now is hurting my feelings. That topic (my wrinkles, or my, like, total inability to remember my, like, *name!*) is off limits." Then later if your child genuinely wants to explore the topic with you and you feel a real shift in his or her motivation, you can open the subject again.

- If you are faced with your child's concern about your mortality, reassure him or her that you are doing everything in your power to take good care of yourself so that you can be around for a long long time. (Also, refer to pages 141–43 in the chapter on the sandwich generation for suggestions on expanding your extended family as a way of reassuring your child that no matter what happens, there will always be people he or she loves and trusts to look after him.) Then remind *yourself* that there are no guarantees at any age. A thirty-year-old mom has no more certainty than you do that she'll live to a ripe old age. And while it's true *statistically* that she'll be around for her twelve-year-old longer than you will be for yours, life throws curve balls, and believing otherwise is one grand illusion. As the parrot in one of my daughter's favorite videos says: "We just gotta live like there might not be a later."

- Be mindful of the promises you ask your child to make, even in jest. "You'll take care of me when I'm old, won't you?" may be said playfully on your part but received as an enormous responsibility in a deep, quiet place in the heart and mind of your child. If you and your child have made any of these agreements, find a suitable time to air them and, if appropriate, to renegotiate them.

- I have spoken with several grown children of first-time older parents who expressed a feeling of inadequacy they had growing up: mom waited so long to have or adopt them, and had such longing and loneliness before their arrival, how could they ever live up to being so special? While it's wonderful to let your child know just how wanted she or he truly was and the lengths you went to to become a parent, remain sensitive to the subtle burden of responsibility for your fulfillment that your child might inadvertently wind up carrying.

- If your child is focusing on the negatives of having an older parent, help them to look through a positive lens. My daughter is a highly verbal, mentally acrobatic nonstop talker. I have often thought that the universe knew exactly what it was doing when it placed her in the arms of a forty-four-year-old woman who had miscarried five times. Lately when she starts griping about my fatigue, I remind her that the advantage of having me for a mom is that I have the patience (read: I'm sitting down a lot) to listen to everything she says and to help her develop all the verbal gifts that might have gotten lost in the shuffle with a younger mom and three siblings. This is called "reframing reality," and it is a constructive alternative to telling her that a younger mother would have cut her tongue out by now.

- It's not uncommon for a child to say, "I'm having kids as soon as I can because I don't want my children to be in the situation I'm in." This is a perfect time to join forces with them rather than try to convince them otherwise. Saying something like "I'd love that. There really is something to be said for having kids at an earlier age, isn't there?" usually diffuses the ticking time bomb.

- And finally, it helps to acknowledge to yourself and to your child that there are definite pros and cons that come with the turf of having an older mother. When your child is old enough to begin expressing some of these feelings, help him or her by getting them their own Journey Book. Make up a box or a basket with the book, colored pens or pencils, a glue stick, scissors, stickers. Guide your child in simple collage or writing exercises: What I think is great about having an older mom; what I hate about having an older mom. Paste in photos that capture some of the memorable times you've shared together. Once your child has the feel for the huge range of emotion and creativity this book can hold, let them know that from here on out unless they ask for your input, the contents are private, for their eyes only. Help them to acknowledge and accept their feelings, and to find ways of expressing themselves creatively no matter what the world dishes up. These are, after all, just a few of the great gifts we can offer our children as first-time moms over forty.

The Journey Book

Wisdom from the Heart

The following questions are Things to Think About. When you have the time, spend fifteen minutes writing about each of them in your Journey Book. You may want to save enough space after each of your answers to come back and respond to them again at another time and in another mood, as your relationship with your child passes through inevitable changes.

1. How do you feel when your child refers to you as "old"?

2. When you were growing up, did you think of your parents as old or old-fashioned? Why? Are there similarities between your feelings about your parents and your child's feelings about you?

3. What do you think and feel about the parents of your child's peers?

4. What are the gifts you bring to parenting your child as an older mother?

Epilogue

So here we are at the end of the book, but very much in the middle of our lives. For the most part we knew what we were doing when we postponed motherhood: The Women's Movement opened doors we wanted to walk through, we longed to leave small towns and travel, we sought higher education and professions that had previously been an exclusive male domain, we waited—and waited—for the right partner.

What we discovered as we entered motherhood for the first time in our forties were joys and challenges we never could have imagined: the intimacy of nurturing and bonding with children, the pleasure of expanding our identity from individual to family member, and a sense of peace and maturity as we learned to weed out the trivial from the true priority at work and at home.

And the challenges? Facing the fact that we are often so tired that flossing our teeth seems—and *is*—a major accomplishment; navigating through the minefield of our youth-worshipping culture with our self-esteem intact; juggling responsibilities to our careers, aging parents, and young children; and struggling to find shelter from the relentless hormonal storms that blow in without warning.

Yet despite all these challenges, every woman I interviewed for this book affirmed the fact that the delights outweighed the

179

disadvantages. Whatever difficulties parenting at midlife presents to us, they are more than compensated for by a greater sense of contentment and self-awareness and the sheer joy of fulfilling our heart's desire to become a mother.

But still we are subjected to unsettling shock:

- We are shocked when we discover with horror that our kids find us ridiculously old-fashioned.

- It's a shock to enter perimenopause shortly after we finish breastfeeding.

- We are shocked when we are offered a senior's discount at the grocery store.

- We face the shock of losing our parents while we are still tending to our toddlers.

- It's a shock to face the inevitable reality that the body ages even as the spirit remains young.

Many of us struggle with these changes and see them as an awful limitation imposed on us just at the very moment we most need our youth. But rather than feeling penalized by fate, I believe older first-time mothers have the unique opportunity to undergo a spiritual development and transformation in the face of these challenging circumstances. Shock has the potential to loosen us from the rock of convention we may have been clinging to and gives us the rare opportunity to cast off commonly held viewpoints so that we may seek the truth within ourselves. Shock has the potential to help us see our children, parents, and partners from a new perspective and to radically readjust our priorities. These waves of shock may be damaging to the ego, but they are always good for the soul. From this perspective, if anything you have read in this book has unsettled you, I hope that it leads you to see whatever limitations fate may have placed upon you as an opportunity to grow.

Writing this book has taught me that I will never be the perfect parent I hoped I would be, but that I have the capacity to do better every day. This desire to be the best we can for our children is strong in older mothers and is truly one of the greatest assets we bring to parenting. A hundred thousand times we lose our tempers, our perspective, our tranquility. A hundred thousand and one times we stand up and try again.

If you have a story you would like to share, or if you want more information about setting up a First-Time Moms over Forty support group in your area, please write to me at:

P.O. Box 31644
Santa Fe, New Mexico 87594-1644

Curriculum

For many first-time mothers over forty, spending time together in a women-only setting is a relief. It's a place to hear the stories of other women and say, "That happened to you too? I thought I was the only one!"

The following is an outline for an eight-week curriculum that has proven to be successful in my First-Time Moms over Forty support groups. Hopefully it will help you structure your own. At the end of the curriculum, you will also find an ad you can place in your local paper seeking first-time older moms for the group, and several suggestions on how to get the word out about the group—free—in newspapers and on the radio.

WEEK ONE: Introduction

This is the week to introduce yourselves and to establish ground rules. These rules may be photocopied and passed out to each member.

Rule Number One: "Whatever we say here stays here." That means that everyone's sharing is held in *absolute* confidentiality. It's not okay to mention even the smallest detail of someone else's story outside of the group, even casually. It's amazing how many people who know people know people.

Rule Number Two: It's essential that group members hold

off phoning each other or meeting with each other socially until the group is over. There will be plenty of time later to form friendships and alliances. Based on my personal experience, outside contact while the group is in progress damages the cohesiveness and feeling of safety of all the members.

Rule Number Three: The group is not a place to heal or resolve any deep emotional issues about our families or about each other. If these issues get stirred up in the course of the group, I suggest that the member(s) seek out individual counseling.

Rule Number Four: Group members are encouraged to share their experience in nonjudgmental "I" statements. These statements can be either points of identification or differences with what another member is saying, but they are always put in terms of a person's *own* experience. Use, "When you say . . ., I feel . . .," not, "That's wrong. You should. . . ." It is not appropriate to give advice or impart an analysis of what someone else may have done, said, or felt.

Once everyone has read over and agreed to the rules, the rest of the meeting can be devoted to getting to know each other. Give each member equal time introducing herself, specifically sharing the story of how she came to motherhood over forty, rather than at twenty or thirty. At the end of the evening, suggest that everyone bring a photograph of herself that represents the life she led B.C.—Before Children—and a journal or notebook to write in.

Week Two: Putting Yourself on the List

This group and each subsequent one begins with a brief check-in. Members go around the circle and take two to three minutes each to talk about "what's most on my mind this week," or to describe herself in four adjectives ("tired, tired, tired, and tired" is acceptable). Again, the purpose isn't to work through deep feelings, it is to take the pulse of the group.

The next fifteen minutes is spent showing each other the photos everyone brought of themselves before they had their children. Next, members are encouraged to spend ten to fifteen minutes writing in their journals about the things—people, places, shopping trips, travel, studies, sports, solitary adventures that recharged and replenished them *before* motherhood. *Nothing* is too trivial. The interests and pleasures each woman identifies for herself become food for thought for the rest of the evening. Group members are encouraged to talk about how to realistically create more time for themselves to enjoy these things and how to "put themselves on the list" of the people they regularly nurture. In closing, each member is encouraged to write a private commitment to herself to incorporate one of these nourishing acts from her former life into her busy current life at least once a week.

Week Three: Empowerment and Aging

The group begins, as always, with a two- to three-minute check-in from each member—"what's most on my mind this week." The topic tonight is aging and what happens when a first-time older mother notices that most of the other mothers in her child's class or at the playground are ten to fifteen years younger than she is. The discussion might include, but isn't necessarily restricted to, how our youth-worshiping culture affects our self-esteem, being mistaken for our child's grandmother, perimenopause (and what is it, anyhow?), and sex after midlife motherhood. Members may talk about the difference between our culture, which places no value in the wisdom of its elders, and other societies where elders are revered. Discussion includes ways to share the wisdom that comes with aging and how to nurture the sacred spiritual life of the community.

WEEK FOUR: Promises and Bargains

The evening begins, as always, with a group check-in. Many of us made promises and bargains before we became mothers: "I promise if I am allowed to have a child I'll never yell. I'll always be a patient, loving, self-sacrificing mother." Once the reality of motherhood sets in, we know in a flash that the reason Mother Teresa was a saint was because she didn't have any kids. We inevitably break our promises and then live with the fear that we will be punished with the loss of our child. Add to this the fact that as older moms we know only too well what can happen to children out in the world, and you end up with a serious case of overprotectiveness and hypervigilence. It is useful for members who are suffering from the guilt pangs of broken promises and bargains to use this night as a safe place to explore this topic.

Use the second half of the evening to discuss the necessity of setting healthy limits and boundaries with children. Older moms often confuse setting limits with a lack of love, but kids need healthy limits to thrive and grow. And besides, when the child who perceives his or her treasured status as the much beloved, pampered only child begins to believe she's exempt from rules and consequences, she soon becomes the kid no one else wants to play with.

WEEK FIVE: Balancing Work and Motherhood

Check-in. This night is devoted to members talking about their successes and struggles as they seek to balance parental responsibilities with career goals. The discussion may expand to include the social and political issues facing women who seek to create a balanced life in a society that devalues motherhood, provides little adequate childcare, and equates personal value with income earned.

WEEK SIX: The Sandwich Generation

Check-in. Older mothers are sandwiched between their older, often ailing parents, and their young children. It's common for an older mom to feel sadness and disappointment because her parents are too old to provide help with the grandchildren and frustration as she struggles to meet both the needs of her parents and her children even as she ignores her own. This evening is devoted to women sharing their experiences as members of the sandwich generation and suggestions on ways to prevent caretaker burnout.

WEEK SEVEN: Creating Community Support

Check-in. Women share leads for finding good childcare, an absolute necessity if there is to be any quality time with oneself or one's partner. Other community-building ideas to be explored include creating "new" families with friends and neighbors who may be willing to function as aunties, uncles, and even grandparents, and starting a neighborhood-run parent cooperative/rotating drop-in center for kids.

WEEK EIGHT: **Potluck and Recap**

Check-in. Each member brings a dish to share. No calorie or carbohydrate counting allowed. Women are encouraged to share what they've gained from the group and what they hope to take with them in terms of new habits and commitments, and new ideas for networking and community building. At this time it is appropriate for women to exchange phone numbers and, if they wish to, plans for extending mutual support to each other now that the group is ending. This meeting closes with the women standing in a circle and holding hands while they silently send prayers of gratitude and best wishes to each other and to all mothers worldwide who seek to do their best for themselves and their families.

Finding Group Members

The following is an ad I ran in a local newspaper over three years ago. A lot of women must have tucked the ad away in a safe place, because I'm still getting calls from it to this day.

> FIRST-TIME MOMS OVER 40
> WERE YOU OVER 40 WHEN YOU HAD YOUR FIRST CHILD?
> If so, I invite you to be part of an eight-week support group
> to explore the complex and demanding physical, emotional,
> and spiritual issues that come with raising children as
> mature women. For more information, contact (name) at
> (phone number).

Running ads like this are costly. I soon discovered that I could place items in what my local paper calls "Community Service Announcements" or "Calendar Listings" for free because there was no charge to participate in the group. The following is a sample community service announcement that drew many responses:

First-Time Moms over 40: Support group forming to explore the complex and demanding physical, emotional, and spiritual issues that come with raising children as mature women. 8 weeks. Contact (name) at (number).

When your phone begins to ring and women want to know more about the group, explain briefly the topics that will be covered. Find out which day and time is most convenient for the majority of people, and set about finding a meeting room to accommodate your needs. I have found that meeting for approximately two hours each week works best. A group of six to eight women is the maximum size. This allows everyone time to share openly without feeling rushed. I recommend finding a neutral place to hold the meetings rather than someone's home where interruptions are inevitable. Churches and libraries often have meeting rooms that are free or that rent for a small cost that can be divided up among members.

It has been my experience that the local talk radio show is an excellent way to attract potential group members. While it may sound intimidating to phone up the local station and ask to speak with the producer of the talk show, in reality it is his or her job to fill the airwaves everyday with someone who can carry on a reasonably intelligent conversation on something of interest to the community. Introduce yourself and tell him or her about the group you are starting. Believe me, they'll know it's interesting. You'll probably be invited on for a five- to ten-minute segment. During that time, you'll be asked questions about your experience as a first-time mom over forty and why you're starting the group. Don't forget to give out your phone number *several* times. Write it on an index card so the host can give it out too. Keep your humor and your wits about you, and it will be over quicker than you can read *Goodnight Moon.*

Resources

The following is an eclectic list of resources, gathered over the years, that can shed additional light on many of the topics in this book.

Adoption and Infertility

Fleming, Ann Taylor. *Motherhood Deferred: A Woman's Journey*. New York: G. P. Putnam's Sons, 1994.

Glazer, Ellen Sarasohn. *Experiencing Infertility: Stories to Inform and Inspire*. Rev. ed. San Francisco: Jossey-Bass, 1998.

————. *The Long-Awaited Stork: A Guide to Parenting after Infertility*. San Francisco: Jossey-Bass, 1998.

Pavao, Joyce Maguire. *The Family of Adoption*. Boston: Beacon Press, 1998.

Adoptive Families of America (AFA)
3333 Highway 100 North
Minneapolis, MN 55422
(800) 372-3300
www.adoptfam.com

Families with Children from China (FCC)
P.O. Box 274
Boston, MA 02258
www.fwcc.org

Families for Russian and Ukrainian Adoption (FRUA)
P.O. Box 2944
Merrifield, VA 22116
(703) 560-6184
www.frua.org

Latin American Adoptive Families (LAAF)
211 Turner Road
East Falmouth, MA 02536
www.marisol.com/laaf/laafhome.htm

National Adoption Information Clearinghouse (NAIC)
5640 Nicholson Lane, Suite 300
Rockville, MD 20852
www.calib.com/naic

National Resource Center for Special Needs Adoption
16250 Northland Drive, Suite 120
Southfield, MI 48075
(248) 443-7080
www.spaulding.org

Parent Network for Post-Institutionalized Children (PNPIC)
P.O. Box 613
Meadowlands, PA 15347
(724) 222-1766
www.pnpic.org

Resolve
1310 Broadway
Somerville, MA 02144-1779
(617) 623-1156
www.resolve.org

Age and Health

Boston Women's Health Book Collective. *The New Our Bodies, Ourselves.* New York: Simon & Schuster, 1992.

Doress, Paula Brown, and Diana Laskin Siegal. *Ourselves, Growing Older.* New York: Simon & Schuster, 1987.

Gittleman, Ann Louise. *Before the Change: Taking Charge of Your Perimenopause.* San Francisco: Harper San Francisco, 1998.

Kelder, Peter. *Ancient Secret of the Fountain of Youth.* New York: Doubleday, 1998.

Northrup, M.D., Christiane. *Women's Bodies, Women's Wisdom: Creating Physical and Emotional Health and Healing.* New York: Bantam Books, 1995.

Poggrebin, Letty Cottin. *Getting Over Getting Older*. New York: Little, Brown & Co., 1996.

Reichman, M.D., Judith. *I'm Too Young to Get Old: Health Care for Women after Forty*. New York: Times Books, 1996.

Rountree, Cathleen. *On Women Turning Forty*. Freedom, CA: Crossing Press, 1991.

———. *On Women Turning Fifty*. San Francisco: Harper San Francisco, 1994.

Careers

Chira, Susan. *A Mother's Place: Taking the Debate about Working Mothers beyond Guilt and Blame*. New York: Harper Collins, 1998.

Godfrey, Joline. *Our Wildest Dreams: Women Entrepreneurs Making Money, Having Fun, Doing Good*. New York: Harper Business, 1992.

Hochschild, Arlie. *The Second Shift*. New York: Viking, 1989.

———. *The Time Bind*. New York: Metropolitan Books, 1997.

Orman, Suze. *The 9 Steps to Financial Freedom: Practical and Spiritual Steps So You Can Stop Worrying*. New York: Crown Publishers, 1997.

Saltzman, Amy. *Down-Shifting: Reinventing Success on a Slower Track*. New York: Harper Collins, 1991.

Sher, Barbara. *It's Only Too Late If You Don't Start Now*. New York: Dell Publishing, 1998.

Working Mother magazine
List of top 100 women-friendly companies
www.workingmother.com

Caregiving

Berman, Claire. *Caring for Yourself While Caring for Your Aging Parents: How to Help, How to Survive*. New York: Henry Holt, 1996.

Illardo, Ph.D., LCSW, Joseph, and Carole Rothman, Ph.D. *I'll Take Care of You: A Practical Guide for Family Caregivers*. Oakland, CA: New Harbinger, 1999.

The American Association of Homes
and Services for the Aging (AAHSA)
901 E Street NW, Suite 500
Washington, DC 20004-2011
(202) 783-2242
www.aahsa.org

California Gray Bears
2710 Chanticleer Avenue
Santa Cruz, CA 95065
(831) 479-1055

Children of Aging Parents (CAPS)
1609 Woodbourne Road, Suite 302-A
Levittown, PA 19057-1511
(215) 945-6900 / (800) 227-7294

Family Caregiver Alliance
(800) 445-8106
www.caregiver.org

The National Academy of Elder Law Attorneys (NAELA)
1604 North Country Club Road
Tucson, AZ 85716
(520) 881-4005
www.naela.com

The National Alliance for Caregiving (NAC)
4720 Montgomery Lane, Suite 642
Bethesda, MD 20814
(301) 718-8444
www.caregiving.org

The National Association for Area Agencies on Aging/Eldercare
Locator
(800) 677-1116
www.aoa.dhhs.gov
www.aahsa.org

The National Association of
Professional Geriatric Care Managers
1604 North Country Club Road
Tucson, AZ 85716
(520) 881-8008
www.caremanager.org

National Family Caregivers Association
10400 Connecticut Ave., #500
Kensington, MD 20895
(800) 896-3650
www.nfcacares.org

The Sandwich Generation Magazine
Box 132
Wickatunk, NJ 07765-0132
$14.00 for annual subscription

Caring for Children

Cummings, F.N.P., Stephen, and Dana Ullman, M.P.H. *Everybody's Guide to Homeopathic Medicines: Taking Care of Yourself and Your Family with Safe and Effective Remedies*. Los Angeles: Jeremy P. Tarcher, 1984.

Herscu, N.D., Paul. *The Homeopathic Treatment of Children*. Berkeley, CA: North Atlantic Books, 1991.

Pipher, Ph.D., Mary. *Reviving Ophelia: Saving the Selves of Adolescent Girls*. New York: Ballantine Books, 1994.

East Bay Moms
6000 Contra Costa Road
Oakland, CA 94618
(510) 653-7867

Journaling

Lamott, Anne. *Bird by Bird: Some Instructions on Writing and Life*. New York: Doubleday, 1994.

Metzger, Deena. *Writing for Your Life: A Guide and Companion to the Inner Worlds*. San Francisco: Harper San Francisco, 1992.

Menopause

Andrews, Lynn V. *Woman at the Edge of Two Worlds: The Spiritual Journey through Menopause*. New York: Harper Collins, 1993.

Bolen, M.D., Jean Shinoda. *Crossing to Avalon*. San Francisco: Harper Collins, 1995.

Horrigan, Bonnie J. *Red Moon Passage: The Power and Wisdom of Menopause.* New York: Harmony Books, 1996.

Lee, M.D., John R. *What Your Doctor May Not Tell You about Menopause.* New York: Warner Books, 1996.

Northrup, M.D., Christiane. *The Wisdom of Menopause.* New York: Random House, 2001.

Sheehy, Gail. *Menopause: The Silent Passage.* New York: Random House, 1992.

Sumrall, Amber Coverdale, and Dena Taylor, eds. *Women of the 14th Moon: Writings on Menopause.* Freedom, Calif.: Crossing Press, 1991.

Weed, Susun. *Menopausal Years the Wise Woman Way: Alternative Approaches for Women 30–90.* Woodstock, NY: Ash Tree Publishing, 1992.

Saliva Testing for Accurate Hormone Levels
Aeron LifeCycles Laboratory
1933 Davis Street, Suite 310
San Leandro, CA 94577
www.aeron.com

Diagnos-Techs, Inc.
P.O. Box 58948
Seattle, WA 98138-1948
(425) 251-0596
Ask for the name of a practitioner in your area who works with this lab.

Transitions for Women
621 Southwest Alder, Suite 900
Portland, OR 97205
(800) 888-6814

Multiples

Center for Loss in Multiple Birth (CLIMB)
c/o Jean Kollantai
P.O. Box 91377
Anchorage, AK 99509
(907) 222-5321
www.climb-support.org

National Organization of Mothers of Twins Club
P.O. Box 438
Thompson Station, TN 37179-0438
(615) 595-0936
www.nomotc.org

The Triplet Connection
P.O. Box 99571
Stockton, CA 95209
(209) 474-0885
www.tripletconnection.org

Twins Online
www.egroups.com/group/twins-on-line
www.twinsadvice.com
www.twinslist.org

Psychology and Mythology

Bolen, M.D., Jean Shinoda. *Goddesses in Everywoman: A New Psychology of Women.* San Francisco: Harper & Row, 1984.

Chinen, M.D., Allan B. *Once Upon a Midlife: Classic Stories and Mythic Tales to Illuminate the Middle Years.* New York: Jeremy P. Tarcher, 1992.

Crittenden, Danielle. *What Our Mothers Didn't Tell Us: Why Happiness Eludes the Modern Woman.* New York: Simon & Schuster, 1999.

Estes, Ph.D., Clarissa Pinkola. *Women Who Run with the Wolves: Myths and Stories of the Wild Woman Archetype.* New York: Ballantine Books, 1992.

Swiggart, Ph.D., Jane. *The Myth of the Perfect Mother: Parenting without Guilt.* Chicago: Contemporary Books, 1998.

Viorst, Judith. *Necessary Losses: The Loves, Illusions, Dependencies and Impossible Expectations That All of Us Have to Give Up in Order to Grow.* New York: Fawcett Gold Medal, 1986.

Single Parenting

Mattes, C.S.W., Jane. *Single Mothers by Choice: A Guide for Single Women Who Are Considering or Have Chosen Motherhood.* New York: Times Books, 1994.

Parents without Partners, Inc.
1650 South Dixie Highway, Suite 510
Boca Raton, FL 33432
(561) 391-8833
www.parentswithoutpartners.org

Single Mothers by Choice
c/o Jane Mattes, C.S.W.
Box 1642
Gracie Square Station
New York, NY 10028
(212) 988-0993
www.parentsplace.com/family/singleparent

Spiritual Inspiration and Renewal

Anthony, Carol K. *A Guide to the I Ching*. Stow, MA: Anthony Publishing, 1988.

Artress, Ph.D., Lauren. *Walking a Sacred Path: Rediscovering the Labyrinth as a Spiritual Tool*. New York: Riverhead Books, 1995.

Bialosky, Jill, and Helen Schulman. *Wanting a Child*. New York: Farrar, Straus & Giroux, 1999.

Bly, Robert, trans. *The Kabir Book: Forty-Four of the Ecstatic Poems of Kabir*. Boston: Beacon Press, 1977.

Breathnach, Sarah Ban. *Simple Abundance: A Daybook of Comfort and Joy*. New York: Warner Books, 1995.

Chodron, Pema. *Start Where You Are: A Guide to Compassionate Living*. Boston: Shambhala, 1994.

———. *When Things Fall Apart: Heart Advice for Difficult Times*. Boston: Shambhala, 1997.

———. *The Wisdom of No Escape*. Boston: Shambhala, 1991.

The Dalai Lama, His Holiness. *The Art of Happiness*. New York: Riverhead Books, 1998.

Kabat-Zinn, Jon. *Full Catastophe Living: Using the Wisdom of Your Body and Mind to Face Stress, Pain and Illness*. New York: Dell Publishing, 1990.

Kornfield, Jack. *A Path with Heart: A Guide through the Perils and Promises of Spiritual Life*. New York: Bantam Books, 1993.

Lamott, Anne. *Operating Instructions: A Journal of My Son's First Year.* New York: Pantheon Books, 1993.

———. *Traveling Mercies: Some Thoughts on Faith.* New York: Anchor Books, 1999.

Levine, Stephen. *A Gradual Awakening.* Garden City, NY: Anchor Books, 1979.

———. *Who Dies?* New York: Doubleday, 1982.

———. *A Year to Live: How to Live This Year As If It Were Your Last.* New York: Bell Tower, 1997.

Lindbergh, Anne Morrow. *Gift from the Sea.* New York: Vintage Books, 1991.

Moyne, John, and Coleman Barks, trans. *Open Secret: Versions of Rumi.* Putney, VT: Threshold Books, 1984.

Oliver, Mary. *New and Selected Poems.* Boston: Beacon Press, 1992.

Pert, Ph.D., Candace B. *Molecules of Emotion.* New York: Scribner, 1997.

Remen, M.D., Rachel Naomi. *Kitchen Table Wisdom: Stories That Heal.* New York: Riverhead Books, 1996.

Wilber, Ken. *Grace and Grit.* Boston: Shambhala, 1993.

Website Resources

www.9to5.org
www.becomingtheparent.com
www.caregiver.org
www.caregiving.com
www.midlifementor.com
www.midlifemommies.com
www.nfcacares.org
www.parentsplace.com
www.power-surge.com
www.salon.com
www.theparentclub.com
www.workingfamilies.berkeley.edu
www.workingmother.com
www.WorkingWoman.com

Index

Clomid, 85, 87
Community support, 76, 141–43, 187.
   See also Support; Support groups
Concentration, lack of, 45
Cosmetic surgery, 26

D

Dalkon Shield, 118
Depression, 47
DES, 113
Dieting, 27
Dinnertime, 65–66
Downshifting, 22–23

E

Eggs
   deterioration of, with age, 79, 81–82
   donors, 83, 86, 96
   drugs stimulating production of, 85
   lifetime quota of, 79
Emotions
   ambivalent, 35–39, 52–53
   "negative," 143–44, 147
Empowerment
   Journey Book exercise on, 31–32
   as support group topic, 185–86
Endorphins, 27
Exercise, 28–29
Expectations, scaling back, 44–47

F

Face-lifts. *See* Cosmetic surgery
Families for Russian and Ukrainian
   Adoption (FRUA), 116, 191
Families with Children from China
   (FCC), 116, 191
Family
   broadening definition of, 142–43
   extended, 70, 141–43
   rituals, 65–66
   "second-batch," 149–64

Fatigue
   coping with, 28, 44–48
   feelings of, 1–2, 10, 35, 170–71
Fertility drugs, 85, 87–88, 91
Food cravings, 27
Freedom of choice, 11–12
Friendships, loss of, 112
Frozen Embryo Transfer (FET), 86

G

Gamete Intrafallopian Transfer (GIFT), 86
Grandmother, being mistaken for, 20–22
Grandparents, absence of, 142–43
Gray Bears, 143, 194
Greer, Germaine, 12

H

Health resources, 192–93
Heart palpitations, 15
Help. *See also* Support; Support groups
   asking for, 110, 147
   live-in, 71
Home, staying at, 66–70
Hormones, 34–35, 44, 48
Hot flashes, 15
Housekeeping, delegating, 144–45
Hysterosalpingogram (HSG) test, 85

I

Incontinence, 16
Infertility, 77–102. *See also* Assisted
   Reproductive Technology; Eggs
   causes of, 81–82, 113, 118
   common reactions to, 79–81
   Journey Book exercises on,
      100–102
   lasting legacies of, 5, 80–81, 94–100
   personal accounts of, 7–8, 82–84,
      86–90, 92–94, 95–97
   resources for, 191–92
Insomnia, 16